Simone de Beauvoir's Political Thinking

Simone de Beauvoir's Political Thinking

Edited by
Lori Jo Marso and Patricia Moynagh

UNIVERSITY OF ILLINOIS PRESS

URBANA AND CHICAGO

© 2006 by the Board of Trustees
of the University of Illinois
All rights reserved
Manufactured in the United States of America
1 2 3 4 5 C P 5 4 3 2 1
∞ This book is printed on acid-free paper.

Library of Congress Cataloging-in-Publication Data
Simone de Beauvoir's political thinking / edited by
Lori Jo Marso and Patricia Moynagh.
p.   cm.
Includes bibliographical references and index.
ISBN-13: 978-0-252-03113-7 (cloth : alk. paper)
ISBN-10: 0-252-03113-x (cloth : alk. paper)
ISBN-13: 978-0-252-07359-5 (pbk. : alk. paper)
ISBN-10: 0-252-07359-2 (pbk. : alk. paper)
1. Beauvoir, Simone de, 1908—Political and social views.
2. Feminism and literature—France—History—20th century.
3. Politics and literature—France—History—20th century.
I. Marso, Lori Jo. II. Moynagh, Patricia.
PQ2603.E362Z885   2006
848'.91409—dc22   2005035190

CONTENTS

ACKNOWLEDGMENTS

BRINGING THIS VOLUME to fruition has been such an enriching collaborative effort for the two of us that, as delighted as we are to see it in print, we are sorry the process has come to an end. We have worked together on this book in Schenectady, in Barcelona, in coffee shops and hotels of the various cities to which we have traveled for the Western Political Science Association conferences, and, most often, in many locations in New York City. Being together in these many venues and having countless conversations has sparked ideas and sharpened our insights on the political issues that have been, and remain, central to our separate and combined work and passions. We hope this volume will extend and deepen the renewed interest in Simone de Beauvoir's life and work, particularly as reflected in her political thinking.

We gratefully acknowledge members of the Western Political Science Feminist Theory Reading Group, especially Judith Grant, who organized a panel of discussants to respond to early versions of our work on Simone de Beauvoir. It was in that forum that many of the ideas in this book were first presented. The group's careful reading and lively exchange on the meaning of Beauvoir's political legacy encouraged us to pursue this volume and seek contributors. Besides offering our own essays, we are fortunate to include here the work of Mary Caputi, Sonia Kruks, Karen Shelby, and Emily Zakin. Earlier versions of Sonia Kruks's essay appeared in *Simone de Beauvoir: 50 Jahre nach dem "Anderen Geschlecht,"* edited by Yvanka B. Raynova and Susanne Moser (Vienna: Institute for Axiological Research, 1999; 2nd ed., Frankfurt am Main: Peter Lang, 2004), 123–40, and as "Panopticism and Shame: Foucault, Beauvoir, and Feminism," in Kruks's book *Retrieving Experience,* copyright

© 2001 Cornell University Press. Emily Zakin's essay is substantially revised from her "Differences in Equality: Beauvoir's Unsettling of the Universal," which appeared in the *Journal of Speculative Philosophy* 14, no. 2 (2000): 104–20. The essays appear with permission of the earlier publishers.

We thank Linda Zerilli and anonymous reviewers of our manuscript for criticisms and comments that greatly enhanced the quality of these essays. We also want to recognize the help of Joan Catapano, editor-in-chief at the University of Illinois Press, in bringing this volume into print. In the final stages of preparation, Carol Betts also provided invaluable assistance. Funding was provided by Union College Faculty Research Fund and the University of Vermont Faculty Professional Development Fund. Finally, while there are many individuals whose insights shaped our thinking, we would especially like to thank Marla Brettschneider, Michelle Chilcoat, Bruce Cronin, Tom Lobe, and Elizabeth Wingrove.

INTRODUCTION: A RADICAL APPROACH
TO POLITICAL THINKING

Lori Jo Marso and Patricia Moynagh

THIS EDITED VOLUME draws on the life and work of Simone de Beauvoir to develop a radical approach to political thinking. We argue that as Beauvoir examined her own life and faced her own situated existence, she introduced a dynamic method of political thinking. This method begins with examples from individual lives and acknowledges them as the very text for understanding and transforming our collective existence. Universal categories are thereby unsettled, yet opportunities to create bonds within common political projects emerge. It is up to us whether or not to embrace them.

We read Beauvoir's account of her own life and the lives of others as a demand to see individuals as always within situation—personal, material, and political. This reading of Beauvoir stipulates that individuals are selves in relation to others, differently located within structures of oppression. We also build on another of Beauvoir's insights. Rather than struggling against systems of injustice, individuals are often tempted to avert action, and the result is simply to do nothing. To resist action in the face of oppression, however, is to deny freedom both for oneself and for others. Individuals may take actions of all kinds, but if action is for themselves alone, freedom is refused. With Beauvoir, we hold that to claim freedom is to reach out toward the world for ourselves and with others. Freedom is never solely an individual accomplishment, and never easily realized. Freedom is *best* achieved in association with others.

Each of the essays within this volume speaks to how Beauvoir conceptualized her own and others' situated existence. Claiming her own embodiment as a woman, Beauvoir turns most frequently to the lives of women to illustrate her political thinking. Beauvoir is most famous for *The Second Sex,* and her work is usually categorized within debates in feminist thought. None of the authors within this volume disputes this placement of Beauvoir's thought. In fact, each draws on it explicitly and extensively. Yet, each author also takes Beauvoir's insights beyond feminism, staking broader claims concerning how Beauvoir's political thinking might be utilized for movements in addition to those for women.

What we identify as Beauvoir's unique contribution to political thinking emerges within these essays around three central themes. First, we embrace the many voices of Beauvoir and see her multivocal perspective as central to her political thinking. While some theoretical framings of Beauvoir's work ask if she adopts either a gynocentric or humanist vantage point, we have consciously resisted such labels under which to categorize Beauvoir's political thinking. While it can be useful to pose such debates, we open up a different path. The authors within this volume work with and develop Beauvoir's insight that it can be quite productive to think against oneself. Setting different of her texts against one another or bringing her own dialogue she carried on with (and against) herself into greater analytical relief are themes pursued by our contributors. Each author engages Beauvoir's multiple voices and grapples with the numerous genres Beauvoir employed across her oeuvre. Her political tracts, novels, philosophical works, interviews, memoirs, and newspaper articles collectively display how Beauvoir consistently challenged herself and challenges us to resist oppression and embrace greater freedom.

Paying close attention to Beauvoir's many voices allows for new insights relevant to contemporary conversations that feminist theorists and others are having, or might have. Moreover, putting Beauvoir into conversation with other contemporary political and feminist theorists, as some in this volume do, illuminates new perspectives on socially and politically important concepts such as freedom, ethics, and human relationships as experienced in a wide array of contexts.

Second, we argue that what we articulate as Beauvoir's method enables a critical analysis of distinct social and political phenomena that is resistant to overgeneralization. Each author works with Beauvoir's texts to reconceptualize universal categories through attending to the particular. These essays locate what is novel in Beauvoir's method by stressing the force of the example, addressing situated existence, and/or engaging lived events, from intimate to intersocietal. Each contributor builds upon the strengths of this method to develop a dynamic and vibrant approach to political thinking.

Each contributor makes broad theoretical claims, but only by way of paying homage to examples from particular lives (Beauvoir's own, that of Djamila Boupacha during her ordeal in Algeria, women in Beauvoir's novels, and the many women to whom she refers in *The Second Sex*). In addition, specific historical events (for example, French colonial intervention in Algeria) are directly addressed as conditioning the broader situation within which Beauvoir and her generation lived.

The essays collected for this volume resist philosophical analysis that fails to attend to circumstances in individual lives. Beauvoir's political thinking, as appropriated by the authors herein, enables investigations of individual lives as historically placed while also calling that very placement into question. At the same time, we interpret Beauvoir's political thought as an invitation to explore larger questions of social existence, including the contrary forces of freedom and destiny. We also find that Beauvoir's approach directs attention to the potential effects any individual's actions might have on political and historical dynamics. Consistent with what we identify as Beauvoir's method, each author within this volume theorizes about current social and political struggles in which each of us is an acknowledged part.

Finally, these essays are in concerted dialogue with Beauvoir on questions of responsibility and political engagement from the individual level to larger social movements. This focus on individual relationships queries Beauvoir's work on questions about the meaning of lived sexuality and how any of us might redefine our sexual existence in more liberating and meaningful ways than modern societies have hitherto allowed. Redefining meaning in liberating ways for women, however, is possible only when women can find better ways to unite across generations and cultures such that our most crippling divisions are overcome. The contributors articulate that each time Beauvoir asks about individuals (herself or others), we are immediately thrust into debates and decisions about larger social, historical, and political forces.

Beauvoir's relationship to Djamila Boupacha, discussed near the end of this introduction and by Shelby and Caputi in the last two chapters of this book, aptly demonstrates the dynamic pull between individual lives and larger forces. We regard Beauvoir's political thinking as a demand to explore and engage the tensions between individuals and their situations, and always to consider the responsibility each individual has to others within the social and political world.

Having articulated three major topics that thematically unite these essays, we render a more general conclusion. Beauvoir's political thinking is a radical call to transform the relations we bear to each other and to ourselves. These essays build upon what we single out as Beauvoir's fundamental challenge to critically confront and transform our social and political lives. Each essay finds in Beauvoir's numerous works a politics that encourages people toward redefinition and social struggle. We read Beauvoir's politics as an appeal to risk action with and for others, and to resist oppression as both individually and collectively experienced.

We can demonstrate Beauvoir's contribution to political thinking most descriptively by turning to the essays themselves and summarizing the chapters as they appear within the volume. Moynagh's essay on exemplary validity and Zakin's on unsettling the universal most vividly address Beauvoir's attention to particularity. By reading Beauvoir's method as a substantive version of Kantian exemplary validity, Moynagh shows a way to find commonalities in women's lived reality where none can be said to exist in advance. Moynagh elucidates the explanatory strength of Beauvoir's phenomenological method, her chief mechanism for analyzing the meaning of lived reality. In taking up the subject matter of sexual difference, for example, Beauvoir makes a vital distinction between ontological claims (for example, that some sort of feminine essence predefines women's way of being in the world independent of any and all experience) and phenomenological claims (for example, that what is truly important is how gender/sexuality is lived or felt by those who experience it).

Beauvoir's method has the distinct virtue of rejecting essentialism while also emphasizing sexed existence as individually experienced. This approach allows Beauvoir to claim her embodied self as a woman, while also calling into question social and political myths that signify her sexuality. Describing lived phenomena, however, if not coupled with a search for greater freedom, may end up endorsing the way things are. For Moynagh, it is precisely this combination of phenomenological description and ethical commitment to freedom that gives Beauvoir's political thinking its emancipatory power.

Complementing this argument by situating Beauvoir within feminist debates over equality and difference, Zakin proposes that we articulate political claims for equality as embodied subjects. She begins by noting that Beauvoir concludes *The Second Sex* by reiterating "there will always be certain differences between men and woman" (Beauvoir 1989, 731). Zakin argues that Beauvoir understands that the self is not only a rational being but also an affective and bodily one, subject to forces and situations that cannot always be mastered. Zakin's essay moves Beauvoir beyond the equality/difference debate within feminism and places her contribution on the terrain of a sexed subjectivity that achieves commonality through projects of freedom.

Zakin traces Beauvoir's positions on equality as they appear on the underside of her writings (on women, on the Marquis de Sade, and on ethics). She finds that Beauvoir's account of the public sphere, and of the relationship between ethics and politics, cannot accommodate any uncomplicated struggle for equal rights, let alone the idea that women must be identified with men in order to be subjects and citizens. When Beauvoir calls for equality for women, she proposes a situation of equal possibilities. She seeks a politics in which each subject's pursuit of herself is unimpaired by any restriction that imposes a pregiven status upon bodies. Beauvoir's provocative suggestion that we think "differences in equality" (Beauvoir 1989, 731) anticipates a relation that maintains the tension between difference and equality productively. It is also consistent with her thesis about subjectivity as nonidentity and ambiguity.

Kruks and Marso in their respective essays turn to the question of how the embodied individual thinks of herself in relationship to inherited social and political configurations. Both authors attend to factors that shape individual consciousness, retrieving sexed subjectivity for the purposes of political transformation. These essays acknowledge embodiment as a conditioning, but not a determining, factor in shaping consciousness.

Reading Beauvoir with and against Michel Foucault, Kruks salvages notions of personal agency and moral accountability that she argues remain "important for any project of emancipatory politics." Kruks contextualizes her discussion of Beauvoir amidst contemporary debates in political theory. She focuses on poststructuralism, with an emphasis on Foucault, and argues that this theoretical vantage point has not advanced fundamentally beyond what Beauvoir's approach already contains. In fact, poststructuralism introduces incoherence not present in Beauvoir's earlier de-essentializing approach.

Kruks argues that there are striking complementarities between Foucault's account of the production of "subjectified subjects" and Beauvoir's account of how one "becomes a woman." However, because Foucault insists on accounting for subjectivity as uniquely a function of disciplinary practices such as panopticism, without regard to the "interiority" of subjectivity, his account remains incomplete. As Kruks shows, it is Beauvoir who better explains just how this process of subjectification is lived, who gets invested in what, and when, and how such subject formation may be challenged. Thus Beauvoir's political thinking does not forsake the desire for freedom, but validates it, situates it, and attempts to realize it more fully.

Marso also foregrounds the desire for freedom on the part of individuals by examining the self's relationships with intimate others, focusing specifically on the need for women to achieve political consciousness. She argues that women might better comprehend, articulate, and act on their desire for freedom, individually and collectively, when acknowledging the full weight of their mothers' lived dilemmas. Marso shows mother-daughter relationships as fraught with difficulties and ambivalence, especially when experienced under conditions that deny women's subjectivity. This is clearly the case under the restraints of patriarchy where women are taught, often by example (looking to their mothers and other women), how to negotiate their desires.

Focusing specifically on women's potential to realize their desires and claim freedom, Marso discusses the contradictory reception of Beauvoir as a "feminist mother." Even as Beauvoir admits the difficulty of living out her freedom under patriarchy, there remains the temptation to elevate her to the impossible status of *the* emancipated woman. Though Beauvoir never embraced this role as feminist icon, Marso finds there is much we can learn from Beauvoir's reflections on her own situation as a woman desiring great-er freedom. If we understand women's commonality as emanating from struggles to win freedom, rather than as essence or fixed identity, women, however differently situated as subjects, may act within political coalition to end their shared oppression.

The final two essays in the volume, those of Shelby and Caputi, focus upon Beauvoir's work as it concerns political action, and its risks in relation to the world at large. These essays demonstrate Beauvoir's argument that we are ethically compelled to do all we can to change oppressive institutions, not only in our closest relations, but more globally as well. Here we witness Beauvoir reaching out to Djamila Boupacha, a young Arab woman wrongly imprisoned, tortured, and raped during the Algerian war for independence (1954–62). By 1962, thirteen years after *The Second Sex* first appeared, Beau-voir had the world's attention and she knew it. This is the year in which Beauvoir publicizes crimes against Boupacha. She aims to raise conscious-ness and inspire political action specifically on Boupacha's behalf. And more broadly, Beauvoir directs attention to this particular case to elicit support within France for Algerian independence.

Within this context of French colonial rule over Algeria during the mid-twentieth century, and while the Algerian struggle for independence was be-ing met by horrific retaliations on Algerian nationals, Beauvoir, Boupacha, and Boupacha's attorney, Gisèle Halimi, attempt nothing short of trans-forming the prevailing world order. The three women plead with the world, particularly French bourgeois opinion, which they expose as dreadfully com-placent. They challenge France to change its ways and end its unjust relationship with Algeria. Significantly, it is Boupacha's body itself that is a primary site of oppression and resistance. Embodiment is essential in this context because Beauvoir and Halimi relate to Boupacha's situation as one only a woman could occupy. Beauvoir conveys this in her introduction to *Djamila Boupacha*. As she begins telling the world about Boupacha, Beauvoir asks:

> Can we still be moved by the sufferings of one young girl? After all—as was delicately hinted by M. Patin, President of the Committee of Public Safety, during an interview at which I was present—Djamila Boupacha is still alive, so her ordeal cannot have been all that frightful. M. Patin was alluding to the use of a bottle on Djamila when he declared: "I feared at first that she might have been violated *per anum,* as was done on occasion with the Viets in Indo-China: such treatment results in perforation of the intestines, and is fatal. But this was something quite different," he added, smiling: clearly nothing of the sort could ever happen to *him.* (Beauvoir and Halimi 1962, 9)

This passage dramatically reveals an emerging solidarity among women who become increasingly conscious of how the world situates them. Well aware of the shame associated with the violation of an Islamic woman's virginity, Beauvoir's *Le Monde* article ("In Defense of Djamila Boupacha," June 2, 1960) boldly declared that Djamila's torturers "forced a bottle into her vagina" (qtd., Beauvoir and Halimi 1962, 65). The violation of this woman's body, she writes "is the concern of every person in France" (197).

The rest of Beauvoir and Halimi's book is an equally intense and sustained appeal to the world, and especially to all French citizens, to realize their complicity within a political structure that encourages systematic atrocities. Beauvoir's writing on behalf of and in defense of Boupacha's fight for her own bodily integrity as well as her people's independence from colonizing France marks the most visible point of her politics as action.

Shelby explores these issues closely by probing how Beauvoir's role as "writer" constitutes a form of political action. The writer must acknowledge her freedom and complicity in the world, while judging the circumstances and opportunities for action she encounters. Shelby discusses how Beauvoir discloses the meaning of her life in relation to others within broader communities. This political insight is developed further by taking up Beauvoir's ideas on freedom and ambiguity. For Beauvoir, Shelby argues, action is not "ethical action unless it gestures in the direction of freedom for all." Shelby explores Beauvoir's work in relationship to that of Hannah Arendt to judge what happens when "action in concert" is inaction. In the final section, she turns to Beauvoir's own actions in relation to the Boupacha case, illustrating that "Beauvoir saw her own role as working primarily through her writing, which would push women and men all over the world to think and to act, and to accept responsibility for their actions and inactions."

Caputi's essay also engages with Beauvoir's highly publicized efforts to bring justice to Boupacha. Caputi addresses the concerns of Frantz Fanon, who was skeptical about the motivations of French intellectuals in taking on a colonial cause. Fanon questioned the extent to which French intellectuals were genuinely concerned about the colonized. He sometimes portrayed their political activities as little more than intellectual solipsism. Additional critics, such as Gisèle Halimi, worried about Beauvoir's perceived lack of emotional investment in Boupacha. Caputi explores these criticisms to confront the political quandaries and risks that arise when we act on the behalf of others.

Caputi exonerates Beauvoir from these charges through an extensive analysis of Beauvoir's ethics. Caputi introduces contemporary debates on the distinctions between "knowing," "acknowledging," and "recognizing" the other. Drawing upon Stanley Cavell, Caputi contends that knowing someone else's pain is a different thing from acting in response to it. She demonstrates the urgency to take action against oppression. One need not know, or even meet, the other who suffers in order to act on that other's behalf. In Caputi's estimation, Beauvoir's actions in response to Boupacha's dilemma illustrate her central point: Beauvoir insists on the necessity for individuals to be aware of their role within structures of oppression as they act in accordance with an ethical commitment that validates freedom.

To explore Beauvoir's involvement with Boupacha's case is a fitting conclusion for this volume. In the introduction to Beauvoir and Halimi's work documenting the torture Boupacha endured, Beauvoir demonstrates the need to take sides, acting politically and with an ethical vision. Her words are worth quoting at length as they illustrate the links she sees between the embodied individual, consciousness, and political action.

> The efforts made on Djamila's behalf would fail in their purpose if they did not create a general revulsion against the sufferings inflicted on her fellow-prisoners—sufferings of which her own case furnished a by no means extreme example. But any such revulsion will lack concrete reality unless it takes the form of political action. The alternatives are simple and clear-cut. Either—despite your willing and facile grief over such past horrors as the Warsaw ghetto or the death of Anne Frank—you align yourselves with our contemporary butchers rather than their victims, and give your unprotest-

ing assent to the martyrdom which thousands of Djamilas and Ahmeds are enduring in your name, almost, indeed, before your very eyes; or else you reject, not merely certain specific practices, but the greater aim which sanctions them, and for which they are essential. In the latter case you will refuse to countenance a war that dares not speak its true name—not to mention an Army that feeds on war, heart and soul, and a Government that knuckles under to the Army's demands; and you will raise heaven and earth to give this gesture of yours effective force. There is no alternative, and I hope this book will help to convince you of the fact. The truth confronts you on all sides. You can no longer mumble the old excuse "We didn't know"; and now that you *do* know, can you continue to feign ignorance, or content yourselves with a mere token utterance of horrified sympathy? I hope not. (Beauvoir and Halimi 1962, 20–21)

Beauvoir's call to political action could not be more powerful. She understands her own embodied existence, as a woman, writer, feminist, and ethical and political thinker, to entail responsibility to fight alongside a woman far less fortunately situated. This is not pity, but more akin to the solidarity that emerges from feminist, embodied consciousness. In the usual terms we might employ (class, race, culture), Beauvoir, Halimi, and Boupacha share little. But as women who desire freedom defined as bodily integrity and improved relationships to all others from most intimate to most global, these three act together to achieve wider political and social transformations. In a contemporary context where debates between "universal" values and "cultural" or "historical" concerns too often obscure the political, social, and economic realities of people's lives, Beauvoir's focus on embodied consciousness and solidarity offers a path toward political action and change.

If ontological claims are ever suspect, as indeed they are in Beauvoir's oeuvre, then we have reason to believe we are capable of redefining ourselves and making positive changes in our lives and how we relate to all others. Beauvoir's texts continue to radicalize as they did a half-century ago. We read Beauvoir's work as delineating a method of political thinking, one that challenges us to confront our lived reality and heighten our awareness of our own position in the social and political world. Armed with this consciousness, we can create opportunities to affirm our interdependency within more just political structures.

As Beauvoir reminds us, "the only sure bonds among men are those they create in transcending themselves into another world by means of common projects" (Beauvoir 1953, 76). It is because we continue to live in a world defined by social and political distress that we look to political thinkers to enlighten us, inspire our actions, and seek alternative realities we have yet to live. We read Beauvoir here as a writer who offers us a radical political vision that enlightens, inspires, and motivates us to enact change.

REFERENCES

Beauvoir, Simone de. 1953. "Must We Burn Sade?" In *The Marquis de Sade: An Essay by Simone de Beauvoir, with Selections from His Writings Chosen by Paul Dinnage.* New York: Grove Press. 9–82.
———. 1989. *The Second Sex.* Trans. H. M. Parshley. New York: Random House.
Beauvoir, Simone de, and Gisèle Halimi. 1962. *Djamila Boupacha: The Story of the Torture of a Young Algerian Girl Which Shocked Liberal French Opinion.* Trans. Peter Green. New York: Macmillan.

1 Beauvoir on Lived Reality, Exemplary Validity, and a Method for Political Thought

PATRICIA MOYNAGH

> I was right to reject essentialism.
>
> —Simone de Beauvoir, *Prime of Life*

> It is clear that no woman can claim without bad faith to situate herself beyond her sex.
>
> —Simone de Beauvoir, *The Second Sex*

IN THE LAST DECADE OR SO, many scholars have turned to Simone de Beauvoir's works with renewed interest. The arguments move from a focus on Beauvoir's original, but often overlooked, philosophical contributions (Kruks, Simons, Bergoffen, Lundgren-Gothlin, and Vintges) to the more dramatic claim that Beauvoir redefines philosophy itself (Bauer). Revisionist scholars continue to enrich our understanding of Beauvoir's legacy by showing that her contributions, already huge, merit greater attention (Moi, Heinämaa, and Ward).

Writing in 1960, as she records her life from 1929 to 1944, Beauvoir identifies herself with an anti-essentialist position. She remembers:

> *I was right to reject essentialism;* I knew already what abuses could follow in the train of abstract concepts such as the "Slav soul," the "Jewish character," "primitive mentality," or *das ewige Weib* [the eternal feminine]. But the universalist notions to which I turned bore me equally far from reality. What I lacked was the idea of "situation," which alone allows one to make some concrete definition of human groups without enslaving them to a timeless and deterministic pattern. But there was no one, outside the framework of the class struggle, who would give me what I needed. ([1960] 1962, 135)[1]

This self-appraisal is announced confidently and with self-conscious vindication that seems almost prophetic of things to come in feminist political
theory debates. But, along with Beauvoir's skepticism about the existence of
Woman is another forceful claim, which appears in *The Second Sex.* There
Beauvoir says: "Surely woman is, like man, a human being; but such a dec-
laration is abstract. The fact is that every concrete human being is always
singularly situated. To decline to accept such notions as the eternal feminine,
the black soul, the Jewish character, is not to deny that Jews, Negroes, women
exist today—this denial does not represent a liberation for those concerned,
but rather a flight from reality. *It is clear that no woman can claim without bad
faith to situate herself beyond her sex.*"[2] Does Beauvoir situate herself without
going beyond her sex *and* reject essentialism? If she manages this, how does
she make it seem possible? How do we judge the more general claims she
makes for and about women?

To address these questions, I focus this essay on examining the method
Beauvoir develops to face up to her own lived reality. I will trace the major
factors that led her to create such a method, which culminates in her writing *The Second Sex,* and then I will argue the merits of this method as valuable beyond helping Beauvoir come to terms with her own sexed existence.
Beauvoir is subjecting to review not only what it means to live as Simone
de Beauvoir (though surely she *is* doing this), but also what it means *to live
as a woman,* be it Simone de Beauvoir or another. As she confronts her own
lived experiences, Beauvoir develops a rigorous method that allows her to
inquire, and in a highly systematic way, about women's situation more generally. Her discovery of situation, of which sexed existence is a part, allows
her "to make some concrete definition of human groups without enslaving
them to a timeless and deterministic pattern."

As those familiar with *The Second Sex* know, Beauvoir questions the idea
of Woman as fixed in mythic understandings and forged by patriarchal cultures. Although Beauvoir consistently brings Woman into question, she never
once questions women's lived reality. As I see it, she does not question this
because her whole project becomes an attempt to describe it as best she can.
Through her descriptions of what women live, she aims to understand the
problems women face in their struggle for freedom.

Beauvoir's method can be related to a particular aspect of Immanuel
Kant's theory of judging. Kant is well known, especially since Hannah Arendt engaged with some of his ideas from his third critique, for making a
distinction between "determinant" and "reflective" judgments. It is the latter
type of judgment that concerns me here. Beauvoir's method is a substan-

tive version of Kantian and Arendtian "exemplary validity." As Kant sees it, determinant judging occurs when any of its practitioners subsume a given particular under a universal concept or rule ("this maple" or "that oak" is a tree). But how are we to judge when there is no rule or idea under which to subsume a given particular? What if the prevailing rule turns out to be a harmful myth? What if women do not incarnate Woman? For Beauvoir, subsuming particular women under the idea of Woman describes the history of patriarchal cultures and its many wrongs against women. If it can be shown that the prevailing rule fails because there can be no a priori rule for women, how should we begin an analysis about women in any case?

As I have started to indicate, and will demonstrate below, Beauvoir will initiate her analysis through describing women's lived reality; but just how it was that she came to recognize the value in this approach is itself worth tracing, and this is what I will do in the first section of this essay. After providing her intellectual development and how she arrived at this descriptive component of her method, I will concentrate on Beauvoir's use of the example as valid for allowing her to make more general claims about women, claims that she could not make otherwise.

Looking for a Way to Face Lived Reality

Beauvoir's life can be read as an attempt to face her lived reality, her drama of self and other. In 1927, when only nineteen and a philosophy student at the Sorbonne, she expressed in her diary the following need: "I must . . . go deeper into the problems that have appealed to me. . . . The theme is almost always this opposition of self and other that I have felt since beginning to live" (qtd., Simons 1999, 217). Beauvoir was drawn to philosophy when she thought it connected up with the reality of her life, and she distanced herself from it whenever it failed to make such links. It often failed. Beauvoir has very scornful words for most philosophers because she thinks they tend to ignore, rather than acknowledge, lived reality. For Beauvoir, acknowledging lived reality will ultimately mean facing the ambiguity of the human condition. Individuals assert themselves as subjects in the world through their intentions, but they also experience themselves as things "crushed by the dark weight of other things" ([1947] 1948, 7).

Beauvoir characterizes the human condition as such in 1947, and with this claim comes one of the harshest indictments of philosophers. Beauvoir writes in *The Ethics of Ambiguity:* "As long as there have been men and they have lived, they have all felt this tragic ambiguity of their condition, but as long as there have been philosophers and they have thought, most of them have tried to mask it" ([1947] 1948, 7). To paraphrase a Marxian adage, I see Beauvoir asserting here that philosophers have masked the human condition in various ways, but the point is to face up to it.

If Beauvoir understands the philosopher's temptation to "bad faith," this is because she herself has succumbed to it. In 1960, at age fifty-two, she is remembering a position she held when she was in her early twenties. She berates herself and Jean-Paul Sartre, her longtime friend and her lover in youth, for their failure to face lived reality, especially in regard to the question of freedom, the clearer articulation of which remained a central goal for both these twentieth-century thinkers.

Beauvoir describes how she and Sartre viewed freedom in their very first years together:

> At every level we failed to face the weight of reality, priding ourselves on what we called our "radical freedom." We clung so long and so desperately to that word "freedom" that it will be as well to make a closer examination of just what we implied by it. There was a genuine enough field of experience for it to cover. Every activity contains its own freedom, intellectual activity in particular, because it seldom repeats itself. We had worked hard; we had been forced, unremittingly, to rediscover and revaluate; we possessed a practical, unimpeachable, intuitive awareness of the nature of freedom. The mistake we made was in failing to restrict this concept to its proper limits. We clung to the image of Kant's dove, supported rather than hindered in flight by the resistant air. We regarded any existent situation as raw material for our joint efforts, and not as a factor conditioning them: we imagined ourselves to be wholly independent agents. ([1960] 1962, 18)

By not facing up to "the weight of reality," Beauvoir experiences the philosopher's tendency to take flight from life itself and therefore the possibility to realize greater freedom. This depiction of "radical freedom" that presupposes "independent agents," who soar above their concrete existence, will prove a nonstarter. Instead of "radical freedom," which ignores the weight of conditions that constrain concrete living subjects, Beauvoir begins to take account of those conditions.

In order to better understand freedom and its possibilities for those who exist, she must face up to the reality of any concrete "situation," whatever it is. In so facing up, she does not abandon her belief in freedom, which she claims both she and Sartre have "a practical, unimpeachable, intuitive awareness." One could even say that her intuitive grasp of freedom's worthiness leads her to be outraged by its denial.[3] The point is not to lose the struggle for freedom but to gain it. Yet, it cannot be won via mere assertions that "radical freedom" belongs to any who claim it. Consequently, Beauvoir validates the reality of "situation" and its relationship to the quest for freedom. While initially drawn to the idea of "radical freedom" as delineated in Sartre's *Being and Nothingness,* she now rebels against it. In time, Sartre will follow her lead, and he too will acknowledge "situation," but he will not take this acknowledgement as much to heart as will she.[4]

In the following excerpt from her memoirs, Beauvoir shares her misgivings about what is increasingly becoming Sartre's, but not her own, account of freedom. Her retrospective characterization of her struggle recalls a mix of self-critique with growing self-assurance that freedom cannot be theorized properly without confronting the lived reality of situated existence. Beauvoir chronicles some of her most significant exchanges on this topic with Sartre, which took place in 1940:

> I had longed for the Absolute too much, and suffered too acutely from its absence, not to recognize in myself that futile drive toward "being" which *L'être et le [n]éant* (*Being and Nothingness*) describes. But what a miserable illusion it is, this search—futile, endless, infinitely repetitive, consuming one's entire life! During the days that followed we discussed certain specific problems, in particular the relationship between "situation" and freedom. I maintained that from the angle of freedom as Sartre defined it—that is an active transcendence of some given context rather than mere stoic resignation—not every situation was equally valid: what sort of transcendence could a woman shut up in a harem achieve? Sartre implied that even such a cloistered existence could be lived in several quite different ways. I stuck to my point for a long time, and in the end made only a token submission. Basically, I was right. But to defend my attitude I should have had to abandon the plane of individual, and therefore idealistic, morality on which we had set ourselves. ([1960] 1962, 346)

Sartre's point, in my view, is that any particular woman in any particular harem could live her "cloistered existence" in quite different ways. Thus, following Sartre, we might imagine one woman in a harem risking the dangers of escape and another hoping to find some refuge in feigning a recurring malady. Yet another might try to exert something of her own "proclivities" by trying to move to the top of some pecking order or deliberately get herself to the bottom, so that she keeps greater or lesser company with the sultan who treats her as *only* a thing, but in whom she may alienate her love anyway. Or not. Another member of the harem might learn how to demean others from the master himself in order to win advantages denied other concubines, including the procurement of one's own slaves. There is also the possibility that these sequestered concubines, trained in giving pleasure to the sultan, seize it for themselves and then freely, if obsequiously, bestow their affection on fellow concubines. Keeping something of their coveted flesh for themselves could become a project in itself. Another harem member might so resent the sultan for subjecting her to this hostile position that she will try to murder her oppressor and rally others, including the oppressed eunuchs, to her cause. Another possibility is to view the situation as insurmountable in which case suicide remains a last option to end this oppression, at least for the woman herself.

Are these imagined possibilities, some of which might have occurred to Sartre when he "implied that even such a cloistered existence could be lived in several quite different ways," no more than orientalizing fantasies? They surely can be read as such, unconnected is the imaginer from any lived actuality of harem life. Nevertheless, Beauvoir's challenge to Sartrean logic is that any of these ways of "transcending" the situation of living in a seraglio reveals the following brute fact. Even if various women stake, risk, or compromise themselves through multiple kinds of assertions, the immense weight of the situation itself is structured to deny women subjective standing. This is the scandal.

Is Beauvoir's position subject to orientalizing conjecture? It certainly may appear strangely ironic for Beauvoir to introduce a woman's placement in a harem as her first and primary example to probe the relationship between freedom and situation. One may charge that as a European intellectual, Beauvoir cannot but speak and gaze from a distance upon a cultural practice that her own society has historically regarded as "other" and less than her own. However, it is not long before Beauvoir's apparently strange and ironic appeal to the harem as initial example to explore a woman's situated existence will lead to her own radical confrontation with herself. As she increasingly faces her own situated existence as a woman, she moves her analysis from what might be deemed mere orientalizing fantasy onto her own terrain where she herself is rooted.

Her move to concentrate upon the more intimately familiar is not to suggest that as Beauvoir faced herself she no longer cared about oppressive predicaments of women living in other cultures. On the contrary, Beauvoir is drawing a connection between her own lived situation and that of other women. What at first seemed only an orientalizing separation now appears as an appeal of linkage, albeit one ravaged by colonial history. In facing her own lived existence as a woman, indeed a relatively privileged life for a woman in mid-twentieth-century France, Beauvoir finds that she is denied her subjectivity. She is afflicted by something she initially posited that other women suffer. Beauvoir instantiates herself as one example among many women who have experienced this denial. That one need not live in a harem to be denied one's subjectivity will become a major rallying point of *The Second Sex*. Beauvoir will endeavor to show that to live as a woman in a patriarchal society, which is to say, society since it has emerged from the Bronze Age, is to experience this lack of subjectivity. The "present enshrines the past," she points out (Beauvoir [1949] 1974, xxiv).

As she considered writing her own life story, she started thinking about what it meant to be a woman. In 1984, Hélène Vivienne Wenzel interviewed Beauvoir and asked why she undertook writing *The Second Sex* in postwar France. Beauvoir responded, "Well, it was because I wanted to talk about myself, and because I realized that in order to talk about myself I had to understand the fact that I was a woman" (qtd., Wenzel 1986, 7). Thus began *The Second Sex*. Its genesis comes out of her desire to write about her own life. But the urge to "explain myself to myself" entailed a "sort of surprise" and "the first thing I had to say was 'I am a woman'" (qtd., Bair 1990, 380). Now she will face up to what this means. But how? She will face up to its meaning by describing "the condition of women in general" (Beauvoir [1963] 1964, 185). In volume 1, she will dedicate her efforts to describing the many myths that survive through history, literature, biological reduction, and the symbolic order that dethrones the mother and replaces her with the laws of the father; in volume 2, she will focus on "lived experiences" of women, which include, as the volume's section and chapter titles say, "The Formative Years" ("Childhood," "The Young Girl," "Sexual Initiation," and "The Lesbian"); "Situation" ("The Married Woman," "The Mother," "Social Life," "Prostitutes and Hetairas," "From Maturity to Old Age," "Woman's Situation and Character"); "Justifications" ("The Narcissist," "The Woman in Love," "The Mystic"); and "Toward Liberation" ("The Independent Woman"). Beauvoir researched and produced *The Second Sex* in roughly two and a half years.[5]

I just noted that Beauvoir sets out to face her lived reality by describing "the condition of women in general." But it must be emphasized that she is choosing to describe the very phenomena of which she herself is an example, precisely because it is not wholly apparent to her how to "understand the fact that I was a woman." Moreover, her descriptions will proceed in a self-conscious historical way since "it is not our concern here to proclaim eternal verities" (Beauvoir [1949] 1974, xxxv). Beauvoir says, "When I use the words *woman* or *feminine* I evidently refer to no archetype, no changeless essence whatever: the reader must understand the phrase 'in the present state of education and custom' after most of my statements" (ibid.). Leaving no doubt that she is employing a phenomenological descriptive method to address her subject, Beauvoir characterizes her undertaking as follows: "Thus, admitting no *a priori* doctrine, no dubious theory, we are confronted by a fact for which we can offer no basis in the nature of things nor any explanation through observed data, and the significance of which we cannot comprehend *a priori*. We can hope to grasp the significance of sexuality only by studying it in its concrete manifestations; and then perhaps the meaning of the word *female* will stand revealed" (10).

But how to study sexuality in its "concrete manifestations"? In the next section, I argue that Beauvoir's turn to the example is the closest she can get to "concrete manifestations," and that attending to these examples of women's embodied existence allows her to "make some concrete definition of human groups without enslaving them to a timeless and deterministic pattern."

Only by attending to examples taken straight from life and experienced by living subjects can she possibly give herself a fighting chance to face reality. That is, with the example as her guide, certain lived and embodied truths may possibly reveal themselves to her. At last, she has produced a philosophy she can inhabit. Or is she bidding adieu to philosophy itself because it is uninhabitable? I ask this question because Beauvoir scholars have persuasively argued that Beauvoir belongs in the pantheon of philosophers. Kruks and Bergoffen, for example, argue convincingly for Beauvoir's original philosophical voice, as distinct from that of Sartre. Simons contends that Beauvoir influenced Merleau-Ponty's later philosophy of "the lived body." She also notes that to make herself a philosopher, "Beauvoir must make philosophy her own, incorporating her passions as well as her reason" (Simons 1999, 215). And, most radical of all, Bauer has argued that by creatively appropriating unto herself philosophers such as Descartes and Hegel, Beauvoir has redefined what should count as philosophy.

However, I do wonder if Beauvoir repudiated philosophy itself, and if her turn to the example of lived and bodily reality is not the best evidence for this disavowal. I am asking if there may not be something about philosophy, try as one might, that takes one from the embodied reality Beauvoir wants to face. When Beauvoir attends to the meaning of her own existence as a woman, she is paying homage to the situated individual who is living the drama of self and other in realms where the stakes are highest: politics, economics, and love. The many attempts to claim Beauvoir as a philosopher might at long last prove a betrayal of not only what she was, but what she wanted to be, a writer, one who says of herself: "I'm a witness. . . . I write it all down" (qtd., Balfour 2001, 10).[6] If Beauvoir does repudiate philosophy, it is not because she's denied entrance to a club that won't have her, however true this remains, but because she deplores the practices of the club.

The next section of this essay brings attention to Beauvoir's use of examples to help her face the reality of her bodily significance and how this relates to the condition of women in general. Her examples are taken from women's lived experiences, including her own. I will argue that through attending to such examples, Beauvoir is attempting to reveal "the significance of sexuality."

That the myth of Woman has wide-ranging and sometimes contradictory effects does not change the fact that it exists. Rather, it shows that different women react to it differently depending upon their own situations. Some women will more readily resign themselves to the myth, or try to justify, even revel in it, usually with disastrous results; others try to adapt to the myth either out of fatigue or because they gain something by doing so, or because they have little choice in the matter; other women will fight to extinguish the myth. In any case, Beauvoir says, "the new woman cannot appear" until women are no longer lured to become incarnations of Woman (Beauvoir [1949] 1974, 809). Because Beauvoir is not interested in discovering absolute truths, but in revealing or disclosing the lived truth of human relations, her turn to the example becomes indispensable.

Beauvoir's Method of Exemplary Validity

It may now appear the height of irony to engage Immanuel Kant with Simone de Beauvoir. But this is precisely what I will do. Many of Kant's critics, including Beauvoir, charge that his philosophy is too formal. But in his third critique, which captured Hannah Arendt's worldly eye, is a wonderful insight, which he calls "exemplary validity." He also discusses the merits of letting the example lead in his first critique. I will now argue that Beauvoir's method is a substantive version of exemplary validity.

Beauvoir does not use the term "exemplary validity" to describe this aspect of her phenomenological method. As indicated above, I borrow the phrase from Kant, who developed the concept for those instances in which he thought we call upon our faculty to judge but do so in the absence of any prior rule to guide us. Later, Arendt would further elaborate upon this need to make judgments when there is no rule under which to subsume particulars but attending to particulars is precisely what we need to do. According to Arendt, something has exemplary validity when it is possible "to see in the particular what is valid for more than one case" (1982, 85).[7]

Beauvoir's examples appear, superabundantly, throughout her writings, and we, her public, can judge for ourselves if we "see in the particular what is valid for more than one case," one woman. Before I further explain why I take Beauvoir's method to be one of exemplary validity, let me first define what Kant and Arendt thought the role the example plays in judgments.

Kant distinguished between two kinds of judgments. Judgments could be either determinant or reflective. Determinant judgments are relatively easy to make because they subsume particulars under some kind of generality where the rule (or schema) is given. For example, one can subsume any particular tree, be it an oak, birch, or maple, under the general concept "tree." My neighbor calls me: "Come look at this unusual tree I just planted," and if in its own way it looks like other trees I have either admired or shaded myself under, then it counts as a tree. I see its trunk or leaves and other distinguishing traits shared by trees in general and I acknowledge "this one" as such. I can think of no one who would argue over this. Or, if someone does, I fail to see the stakes in doing so. It is more like this: I have experienced trees before. My intuition of "this" or "that" tree and my conceptual understanding will hopefully have occasion to combine again in the future, allowing me to experience many more trees in their many delightful varieties.

But if, in the middle of an abstract discussion, a man says to Beauvoir, or to any other woman, "You think thus and so because you are a woman" (Beauvoir [1949] 1974, xviii), this is not an acceptable subsumption. It is not acceptable because these words signal a deep social problem in which men historically dismiss women. Beauvoir says that "it is vexing to hear a man say these words" (ibid.). Such an incident, especially because it recurs, makes of Beauvoir a Woman, rather than allowing her human status as a woman. A whole social and political universe, with deep sexual oppression, is revealed in this one utterance: "You think thus and so because you are a woman." By describing her own experience, Beauvoir also characterizes women's lived predicament in general.

Historically, men have tended to deny women their subjectivity, and then each woman looks for ways to deal with this denial. Depending upon her entire situation, which will vary from one woman to the next because of such factors as racial and social status and class, as well as disposition and character, she will either rebel, reluctantly or more willfully comply, or maybe even try to justify this denial, but with ruinous effects for both herself and others. No woman escapes all of the time. This is why Beauvoir says, "In my view the real task of feminism can only be the transformation of society along with the transformation of women's place in it" (qtd., Schwarzer 1984, 116). To achieve this transformation, women need to see their commonalities arising from their very life situation.

Beauvoir's example illustrates that she is situated in a particular kind of world, one whose inhabitants are fleeing themselves and others by not assuming their freedom. It is in this very same world, though, that her male interlocutor dwells with her, but his situation is different from hers because he is not likely to experience a denial of his subjectivity on account of his sex.

Beauvoir's position is this: she wants to claim her sexed existence but not be defined exclusively by it. Beauvoir puts it this way: "My feminine status . . . is a given condition of my life, not an explanation of it" ([1960] 1962, 292). This is why she finds it unjust if she is reduced to her sex. On the other hand, trying to remove herself from her sexed existence is not a "good faith" option because doing so would also deny her "subjective self." Beauvoir considers her options to respond to the man who has dismissed her as a Woman in their conversation. She says, "I know that my only defense is to reply: 'I think thus and so because it is true,' thereby removing my subjective self from the argument. It would be out of the question to reply: 'And you think the contrary because you are a man,' for it is understood that the fact of being a man is no peculiarity. A man is in the right in being a man; it is a woman who is in the wrong" ([1949] 1974, xviii).

Toril Moi, who examines this dilemmatic situation experienced by Beauvoir, observes that if Beauvoir removes her subjectivity in order to save her intellectual integrity, "it is precisely the fact of having to do that, that makes the situation unfair, unequal, and ultimately oppressive to her" (1999, 215).[8] Moi further points out the difference between a woman wanting to bring her sexuality to the foreground when, for example, physically attracted to another, and "the compulsory foregrounding of the female body at all times, whether it is relevant or irrelevant to the task at hand" (202).[9]

By attending to an example from her own life, Beauvoir sheds light on women's condition in general. Her incidents are none other than hers; they retain their uniqueness and are "singularly situated." But in her particular description of her very own phenomena, she reveals what remains one of women's most fundamental dilemmas and the contradiction that is her life. Thus it is that the "example discloses generality without surrendering particularity" (Arendt 1982, 130).[10] By describing herself, Beauvoir faces up to her lived reality and discloses the greater predicament for women more generally. A very real aspect of Beauvoir's embodiment is that in it, not only is she defined by others than herself—for this Beauvoir thinks is inevitable—but also she, like other women, is "othered" as completely Other.

When this definition becomes a complete reduction, and she is never consulted in the matter, it turns oppressive. And yet each woman, like every human who lives or ever has lived, is embodied, of course. To deny one's embodiment, as, say, Descartes does, is in complete "bad faith" because it is an attempt to escape the reality of one's own fleshly existence with all its ambiguity.[11] When Beauvoir declares, "I am a woman," she is claiming, rather than running from, her embodiment. Remember she believes, "It is clear that no woman can claim without bad faith to situate herself beyond her sex." When she questions the eternal feminine, she challenges the denial of her subjectivity and that she is essentially a Woman.

But just what is Beauvoir revealing by attending to her lived reality if not that of others as well? She maintains that in man's attempt to flee his own bodily reality, he has reduced woman to hers. Beauvoir is discovering that to face reality is to face bodily existence as it is lived. She says, "[I]t is not the body-object described by the biologists that actually exists, but *the lived body of the subject*" ([1949], 1974, xx, my emphasis) and "if the body is not a thing it is a situation" (33).[12]

Beauvoir's analysis makes the body, *the lived body,* central to her analysis. Yet, she does not ignore biological materiality. That is, the biological body cannot by itself convey meaning because this depends upon an interactive process, which of course includes the body, but is not solely dependent upon it for its meaning. Beauvoir says, "Biology is not sufficient to give an answer to the question that confronts us: why is woman the Other?" ([1949] 1974, 77). She says further, "In our attempt to discover woman we shall not reject certain contributions of biology, of psychoanalysis, and of historical materialism; *but we shall hold that the body, the sexual life, and the resources of technology exist concretely for man only in so far as he grasps them in the total perspective of his existence*" (67, italics mine).

But whence comes this denial of women's subjectivity? Beauvoir says it has to do with what is made of women's bodies, rather than with anything essential about them; but she honors physiology as an important component of women's entire situation in the world. She writes, "Woman is determined not by her hormones or by mysterious instincts, but by the manner in which her body and her relation to the world are modified through the action of others than herself" ([1949] 1974, 806). This is an important point to emphasize because many have criticized Beauvoir for either adopting a negative view of women's bodies or treating the body as a thing, rather than concentrating on its lived meaning.[13] I do not read Beauvoir as viewing women's bodies negatively, nor do I see her treating them as things.

I do see this: with her attempt to face her own embodied reality comes the realization that so many others flee from this attempt, but with devastating consequences, especially for women. Beauvoir by no means ignores the sexed body and its physiological functions; in fact, she claims that women's bodies serve as the most profound reminders of life and death. Remember that Beauvoir is trying to face, rather than mask, the reality that she thinks shapes *her* human condition.

So, it is one thing to classify a particular tree under the general concept "tree," but quite another to subsume women under the concept "Woman" when Beauvoir shows that she has been both subject and witness to its wrongs. Beauvoir is not willing to make such a subsumption. Determinant judgments cannot be made in the case of women because there is no rule for all, or if there is one, we cannot know it in advance. More important, that which has for so long tried to pass itself off as a universal rule, ready-made for women, the eternal feminine, has been and remains an outrageous failure because it has mutilated so many lives—men's too, whose real liberation can occur only with that of women.

If not determinant, what about reflective judgments? Might these describe Beauvoir's attempt to disclose women? Remember that unlike determinant judgments, which seek to subsume the particular under the general idea or rule that can be given, and unproblematically accepted, reflective judgments proceed in the opposite direction. They are more from the ground up. Reflective judgments begin with particulars. We make reflective judgments, Kant thought, when only the particular is given and we have no rule or law or idea under which to subsume the particular that we experience. Now, what guides us as we judge under such conditions?

Kant thought the example was key in such instances. Because there is no rule for reflective judging, he said, "Examples are thus the go-cart of judgments" (1965, 178). Without the examples, no judgments. Kant also claims that the most learned can "easily stumble" for lack of examples, and he says such "sharpening of the judgment is indeed the one great benefit of examples" (178). In addition, he says that "judgment is a peculiar talent which can be practiced only, and cannot be taught. It is the specific quality of so-called mother-wit; and its lack no school can make good" (177). Beauvoir seems to follow these Kantian insights. When there is no rule, or the rule has failed us all, let the example lead and guide. Examples become Beauvoir's "go-cart."

To sharpen her judgment, Beauvoir turns to the many examples of women's lived embodiment. She is not sure what rules, if any, she might find in her investigation of attending to these examples. But it seems the only method at her disposal to contest the prevailing rule of Woman by which women are judged, without foreclosing the possibility that her attentiveness to the many examples of women's lived experiences might reveal commonalities among women, when none can be said to exist in advance. In other words, if she makes general claims for women, they will not accord with what the canonical fathers have long decreed but will emerge from the dutiful daughter's attempt to face the reality of her own lived embodiment.

I claim Beauvoir's examples interest us because they transcend themselves yet remain situated. Examples from her memoirs have occurred in time and place even if she does not provide the date, though she usually does. Beauvoir describes experiences that have been lived by actual women, and she situates them in their moment, both in *The Second Sex* and in her fiction. Most original of all, in Beauvoir's concept of the body we find the claim that this is itself a situation, largely dependent for its lived meaning upon what others make of it.[14] Her examples pay tribute to the utter and complete singularity of any one event or life, honoring that "[e]ach one has the incomparable taste in his mouth of his own life" (Beauvoir [1947] 1948, 9). Yet her examples go beyond themselves. For all their specificity, which Beauvoir is intent on preserving, her examples are not contained to themselves because they expose the oppression of women in its "endless variety and monotonous similarity" (qtd., Fraser and Nicholson 1990, 35). If Beauvoir does reveal a commonality among women, as I claim she does, this is because she sharpens her judgments by giving examples their due.

I contend it is possible that Beauvoir's attention to examples from women's lived reality allows her to make credible claims about women's condition in general, but it must be noted that mine is a controversial contention. Eminent readers of Beauvoir have put forth the exact opposite argument. For example, Elizabeth Spelman maintains that Beauvoir discredits herself by actually lodging privilege in her method. Spelman cautions readers of *The Second Sex* not to repeat Beauvoir's mistakes by speaking of one kind of woman's experiences as representative of all.

In my view, Spelman's book *Inessential Woman* serves as a much needed warning to those who care about the oppression of women not to segregate this from other factors of oppression based upon race, class, and sexuality. Spelman is concerned that Beauvoir's work "has both reflected and perpetuated a choice to focus on the lives of some women rather than others" (Spelman 1988, 58). In a critique of Beauvoir, Spelman says, "I think that in de Beauvoir's work we have all the essential ingredients of a feminist account of 'women's lives' that would not conflate 'woman' with a small group of women—namely white middle-class heterosexual Christian women in Western countries. Yet Beauvoir ends up producing an account which does just that" (ibid.).

Spelman claims "we honor her work by asking how such privilege functions in her own thinking" (1988, 77). But I think we honor her work better still if, in seeing its shortcomings, we nevertheless focus on its redemptive possibilities, possibilities that Spelman herself recognizes. Whereas Spelman asks how Beauvoir, who is broadly attuned to issues of race and class oppression, could produce a narrow conception of women's general condition, I suggest that Beauvoir's sensitivity to oppression in its many lived forms leads her to a focus on examples, which is where we ought to keep our focus as well. That Beauvoir sometimes contradicts herself probably has much to do with the oppression of the language she inherits.

Spelman is justifiably concerned that in speaking about "women" and juxtaposing this group to "Negroes" or "Jews," the women in these latter groups get erased. This is, of course, a legitimate criticism. However, it should also be remembered that Beauvoir said about her writing of *The Second Sex,* "I was discovering my ideas as I was explaining them, and that was the best I could do" ([1963] 1964, 191–92). And, as Spelman also notes, Beauvoir was well aware that women "live dispersed among the males" ([1949] 1974, xxii) and what this often means. Through such attachments as "residence, housework, economic conditions, and social standing," women are often "more firmly" linked to men rather than to other women. Beauvoir writes: "If they belong to the bourgeoisie, they feel solidarity with men of that class, not with proletarian women; if they are white, their allegiance is to white men, not Negro women" (ibid.). Beauvoir recognizes these difficult social alignments that continue to work against women as a whole, and she wants to break through them. About her own social position, Beauvoir claims her whiteness and calls it a "curse." Describing her thoughts as she walked through Harlem in 1947, she writes, "And because I'm white, whatever I think and say and do, this curse weighs on me as well. I dare not smile at the children in the squares; I don't feel I have the right to stroll in the streets where the color of my eyes signifies injustice, arrogance, and hatred" ([1954] 1999, 36).[15]

Beauvoir's is a method that does not seek certitudes, but it moves nearer to the truth all the same. This is why her method must rely, as it does, on examples taken straight from life. Such examples will avoid banality and empty clichés because they are simply nonrepeatable. Examples preserve the integrity of the particular event, even when it is quite horrid, and thus attend to reality.

According to Beauvoir's favored method for describing rather than masking reality, one takes examples from everyday lives and then reflects upon them, asking what they reveal. Understanding this aspect of Beauvoir's method goes a long way toward explaining why she consistently fills her texts— whether autobiographical, literary, philosophical, or more explicitly political—with examples from lived experiences. However, if her examples are merely idiosyncratic, they will not concern us because they do not reach out into the world of others or address issues of freedom. They may very well interest us, but not in the way that they do if they have exemplary validity. For this to be the case, her examples must go beyond herself. They will not speak to anybody else otherwise. While retaining their specificity, her examples must address the more general conditions shaping women's lives.

This is Beauvoir's dialogic pitch to her audience: Do you see your life or other women's lived experiences depicted in the examples I present to you? Do you see something of yourself or others in my struggles even though we are worlds apart? If yes, then they have exemplary validity. To the extent that we see within any example she furnishes a similar pattern revealed about our own or other women's lives, her examples are well chosen and valid.

It is not enough to record and describe one's own experiences, an art Beauvoir certainly mastered. Beauvoir once said that many women tell her they are writing their lives. Beauvoir does not discourage them, but she makes a distinction between writing for oneself alone and writing for oneself and others. If one writes only for oneself, this can serve a therapeutic purpose and on that account is recommended (see Schwarzer 1984). But writing about oneself in a way that is socially committed demands an involvement with the fate of others, a love for the world. Beauvoir's writing is political writing because it reaches out to others and asks what is necessary for freedom to be more possible. Beauvoir's writing is not a solitary practice, though it may be carried out alone. This way of writing "for oneself" and "for others" is a profoundly social endeavor, an "appeal" to others for a response.

NOTES

1. Italics in the first sentence are mine. *The Prime of Life* appeared originally as *La force de l'age*, in 1960.

2. This passage appears in *Le Deuxième Sexe* (1949), vol. 1, 13. Italics in the last sentence are mine. The English translation of this passage is from *The Second Sex* (1974), xvi–xvii. I am using a retranslated version of this passage from the original French. There are two reasons for this. First, the second sentence from this passage is misconstrued badly by H. M. Parshley in the only English version of *The Second Sex* now available. Second, the last sentence from this passage is missing altogether in Parshley's translation. Yet, that sentence is integral to my argument that Beauvoir claimed her embodied sexuality. Parshley translates the second sentence from this passage thus: "The fact is that every concrete human being is always a singular, separate individual" (xvi). Compare this with what Simons deciphers: "The fact is that every concrete human being is always singularly situated" (Simons 1999, 158). Simons restores Beauvoir's meaning as the original French reads, "le fait est que tout être humain concret est toujours singulièrement situé." Simons notes other instances of misrepresentation throughout Parshley's translation. For example, Parshley regularly translates *pour-soi* as "in-itself" rather than "*Being* for-itself," which is to invert its technical existential meaning. Simons also alerts readers to the fact that while Beauvoir was careful to use the Heideggerian phrase "la réalité humaine" (human reality), Parshley translates this as "the real nature of man." For a thorough account of the problems with the Parshley translation, see Simons 1999.

3. Some debates focus on Beauvoir's prior ontological commitment to freedom over what Gail E. Linsenbard calls its "practical" dimensions. However, these debates strike me as less important to engage than what emerges once Beauvoir faces the reality of situation. In my view, Linsenbard's analysis is not incorrect, but it is misleading all the same. That is, I do not think that Beauvoir would have reached the method I am arguing is so crucial for feminist political theory if she never descended from the ontological level. Even if we grant that Beauvoir must presuppose a certain integrity to ontological freedom in order to argue so passionately for a liberated world, it is only *when* Beauvoir begins to thickly describe women's conditions, as well as conditions of other oppressed groups, that she discloses revelations that would otherwise remain inaccessible to her and her public. For a forceful argument that situates this debate within the context of genital mutilation of girls and women in Africa and Beauvoir's public denunciation of these atrocities in 1986 as violating human rights, see Linsenbard (1999).

4. For an excellent discussion that takes the reader through Sartre's shift and Beauvoir's influence upon his rethinking of freedom in light of situation, see Kruks (1995).

5. Beauvoir says that *The Second Sex* "was begun in October 1946 and finished in June 1949; but I spent four months of 1947 in America, and *America Day by Day* kept me busy for six months" (qtd., Bair 1990, 380).

6. This phrase is James Baldwin's, which he uses to characterize his own efforts to take account of his embodied life and the world in which he dwells. For an inter-

esting study that argues his writings are phenomenological attempts to describe his lived experiences of race and sexuality, see Balfour (2001).

7. See also Kant (1991, 18 and 151).

8. Both Moi and I make the case for the credibility of Beauvoir's examples which, in their very particularity, instantiate something more general. But, whereas she draws on Ludwig Wittgenstein and Stanley Cavell, I draw on Kant and Arendt in letting the example lead. See her discussion on "Exemplarity" (Moi 1999, 227–37).

9. For a fuller discussion of these issues, see Moi (1999, 190–207).

10. This quotation is taken from Ronald Beiner's interpretive essay in Arendt (1982).

11. I cannot pursue the full depth of her argument here, but Nancy Bauer offers a fascinating case that illustrates how Beauvoir's *The Second Sex* is an attempt to re-write Descartes's *Meditations* from the ground up. See chapter 2, entitled "I Am a Woman, Therefrom I Think," in Bauer (2001).

12. Rather, Beauvoir consistently analyzed the body as a situation. Heinämaa documents that the sex-gender duality does not originate with Beauvoir. Heinämaa reports that the "sex/gender distinction first appeared in the beginning of the 1960s in texts written by a group of American psychoanalysts" (1997, 35, n. 14). She refers to Robert Stoller's key work from this period, *Sex and Gender: The Development of Femininity and Masculinity,* in which he offers a psychoanalytic theory on the formation of transsexual gender-identity. Stoller refers to Freud's essay "A Case of Homosexuality Among Women," where Freud had distinguished three different aspects of homosexuality: the physical, the mental, and the object-choice. Stoller then identifies his concept of gender with the second of these Freudian categories. Feminists of the 1960s and 1970s, among them Millet, Greer, Oakley, and Firestone, then referred to Stoller's work when introducing the sex/gender distinction into their own work. See Heinämaa (1997, 35).

13. For the opinion that Beauvoir adopted a negative view of women's bodies, see, for example, Mary O'Brien (1981), where O'Brien claims that *The Second Sex* undermines women's capacity to reproduce. Similarly, Moira Gatens has taken Beauvoir to task for presupposing that women "simply *are* absolutely Other" due to female biology. See Gatens (1991, 127). Elizabeth Grosz claims that Beauvoir treats the body as a thing, unlike other feminists such as Irigaray, Cixous, Spivak, Wittig, Butler, and many others who are concerned with the lived body. That Beauvoir treats the body as a thing is simply not true, though she says we may experience it as such and indeed this may be inevitable. See Grosz (1994, 15–18).

14. For an excellent discussion on this topic, see Ward (1995, 223–42).

15. It should be noted that she is painfully aware of her privileged situation in her native France and how this benefited but also compromised her. She experiences her own situation with a heavy heart. She says of herself: "I know that I am a profiteer, and that I am one primarily because of the education I received and the possibilities it opened up for me. I exploit no one directly; but the people who buy my books are all beneficiaries of an economy founded upon exploitation. I am an accomplice of the privileged classes and compromised by this connection; that is the reason why living through the Algerian war was like experiencing a personal tragedy. When one

lives in an unjust world there is no use hoping by some means to purify oneself of that injustice" ([1963] 1964, 652).

REFERENCES

Arendt, Hannah. 1982. *Lectures on Kant's Political Philosophy.* Ed. Ronald Beiner. Chicago: University of Chicago.

Bair, Deirdre. 1990. *Simone de Beauvoir: A Biography.* New York: Summit Books.

Balfour, Lawrie. 2001. *The Evidence of Things Not Said: James Baldwin and the Promise of American Democracy.* Ithaca: Cornell University Press.

Bauer, Nancy. 2001. *Simone de Beauvoir, Philosophy, and Feminism.* New York: Columbia University Press.

Beauvoir, Simone de. [1947] 1948. *The Ethics of Ambiguity.* Trans. Bernard Frechtman. New York: Philosophical Library.

———. [1949] 1974. *The Second Sex.* Trans. and ed. H. M. Parshley. New York: Vintage.

———. [1949] 1986. *Le deuxième sexe.* Paris: Gallimard. Vol. 1.

———. [1949] 1986. *Le deuxième sexe.* Paris: Gallimard. Vol. 2.

———. [1954] 1999. *America Day by Day.* Berkeley: University of California Press.

———. [1960] 1962. *The Prime of Life.* Trans. Peter Green. Cleveland: World.

———. [1963] 1964. *Force of Circumstance.* Trans. Richard Howard. New York: Putnam.

Bergoffen, Debra B. 1997. *The Philosophy of Simone de Beauvoir: Gendered Phenomenologies, Erotic Generosities.* Albany: State University of New York Press.

Fraser, Nancy, and Linda J. Nicholson, 1990. "Social Criticism without Philosophy: An Encounter between Feminism and Postmodernism." In *Feminism/Postmodernism.* Ed. Linda J. Nicholson. New York: Routledge. 19–38.

Gatens, Moira. 1991. *Feminism and Philosophy: Perspectives on Difference and Equality.* Bloomington: University of Indiana Press.

Grosz, Elizabeth. 1994. *Volatile Bodies: Toward a Corporeal Feminism.* Bloomington: Indiana University Press.

Heinämaa, Sara. 1997. "What Is a Woman? Butler and Beauvoir on the Foundations of Sexual Difference." *Hypatia* 12, no. 1 (Winter): 20–39.

Kant, Immanuel. 1965. *Critique of Pure Reason.* Trans. Norman Kemp Smith. New York: St. Martin's.

———. 1991. *Critique of Judgment.* Trans. James Creed Meredith. Oxford: Clarendon.

Kruks, Sonia. 1995. "Simone de Beauvoir: Teaching Sartre About Freedom." In Simons 1995, 79–95.

———. 2001. *Retrieving Experience: Subjectivity and Recognition in Feminist Politics.* Ithaca: Cornell University Press.

Linsenbard, Gail E. 1999. "Beauvoir, Ontology, and Women's Human Rights." In "The Philosophy of Simone de Beauvoir," ed. Margaret A. Simons, special issue, *Hypatia* 14, no. 4 (Fall): 145–62.

Moi, Toril. 1999. *What Is a Woman? And Other Essays.* New York: Oxford University Press.

O'Brien, Mary. 1981. *The Politics of Reproduction.* Boston: Routledge and Kegan Paul.

Sartre, Jean-Paul. [1943] 1956. *Being and Nothingness: An Essay on Phenomenological Ontology.* Trans. Hazel E. Barnes. New York: Philosophical Library.

Schwarzer, Alice. 1984. *After the Second Sex: Conversations with Simone de Beauvoir.* New York: Pantheon.

Simons, Margaret A., ed. 1995. *Feminist Interpretations of Simone de Beauvoir.* University Park: Pennsylvania State University Press.

Simons, Margaret A. 1999. *Feminism, Race, and the Origins of Existentialism.* New York: Rowman and Littlefield.

Spelman, Elizabeth V. 1988. *Inessential Woman: Problems of Exclusion in Feminist Thought.* Boston: Beacon.

Vintges, Karen. 1996. *Philosophy as Passion: The Thinking of Simone de Beauvoir.* Bloomington: Indiana University Press.

Ward, Julie K., 1995. "Beauvoir's Two Senses of "Body" in "*The Second Sex.*" In Simons 1995, 223–42.

Wenzel, Hélène Vivienne. 1986. "Interview with Simone de Beauvoir." *Yale French Studies* 72:5–32.

2 Beauvoir's Unsettling of the Universal

EMILY ZAKIN

ONE WAY OF READING *The Second Sex* is as a prolonged meditation on the patriarchal relation between femininity and universality, a relation in which each term is reciprocally defined by its exclusion of the other. By querying the masculine presumption of the universal subject, Beauvoir exposes the limitations and dangers inherent in the Cartesian *cogito* and invites feminists to articulate (theoretically and politically) woman as subject. Such a project would seem conducive to, or at least complementary with, the agenda of much contemporary French feminism, a genre that for all its diverse and fractious positionings can generally be said to negotiate this same conflict. Yet, Beauvoir is more often read in contrast to, or against, the likes of Kristeva and Irigaray than with them.

Although what is called French feminism is less a single definable set of theoretical doctrines than a varying constellation of philosophers, theorists, and writers, it is remarkable that Beauvoir is often understood to be on the outside of this assemblage. Irigaray and Kristeva, perhaps the most prominent members of this coterie (and unlike Beauvoir, not themselves of French origin), both have tense theoretical relations with Beauvoir, recognizing her work as perhaps historically important but nonetheless somehow outmoded. Despite the major differences between Irigaray and Kristeva, the two share similar reasons for this relegation: a training in and commitment to psychoanalysis, and a suspicion of the abstract universal and its repression of difference. Irigaray, for instance, suspects Beauvoir of caring more for a politics of equality based on a masculine standard than for granting "cultural values to femininity" (Irigaray 1993a, 13), and Kristeva in her turn places Beauvoir among the first of three generations of feminism, a generation committed to allocating a place for women within the social and symbolic orders. "Existential feminists," Kristeva writes, "aspire to gain a place in linear time as the time of project and history" (1986, 193). Both of them interpret Beauvoir's project as one destined to reinstantiate a masculine universal under the name of neutrality and reason, and therefore as an evasion of difference and the unconscious. Beauvoir is viewed as rejecting femininity in order to assimilate women to the universal.[1]

Yet Beauvoir concludes *The Second Sex* by reiterating that "there will always be certain differences between man and woman" (1989, 731), and in her analysis of the conundrum faced by "The Independent Woman," she is clear that the conflict between femininity and subjectivity cannot be resolved by the repudiation of her sex, calling this a "mutilation" and maintaining that "to renounce her femininity is to renounce a part of her humanity" (682).[2] Beauvoir is insistent that for woman to be a "complete individual," she must be a "human being with sexuality" (ibid.). Beauvoir understands that the self is not only a rational being, but also an affective and bodily one, a sexed and sexual subject susceptible to forces and situations that cannot always be mastered.[3] In this regard, Beauvoir's reading of Sade (a reading that is itself manifestly influenced by Freud) shows clearly that she rejects the claims of an all-encompassing neutral reason that operates without limit.

For these and similar reasons, recent work in Beauvoir scholarship has raised questions about the reading of Beauvoir as feminist but antifeminine. As Debra Bergoffen has argued (1997), Beauvoir is concerned not only with a politics of equality (though this is an especially prominent theme in *The Second Sex*), but also with an ethics of openness to the other, of alterity and ambiguity, what Bergoffen calls an "erotics of generosity" (36). Bergoffen defends this interpretation of Beauvoir by maintaining that there is a subterranean, "muted" voice at work in her writings, a voice that gives expression to theses that may not be overtly stated, but perhaps exhibit philosophical commitments that the dominant voice occludes. The muted voice is "a legacy of hints" (Bergoffen 1997, 39) and it gestures toward positions that are otherwise and elsewhere than might at first be apparent. Differentiating between the dominant voice of Beauvoir's writing and her muted voice, Bergoffen reminds us that Beauvoir's work is itself sometimes contradictory, and that it does not work out a singular philosophical project.[4] In particular, by helping us to recognize the multiple axes on which Beauvoir is formulating her arguments, Bergoffen's distinction asks us to attend to the ways in which Beauvoir situates women's identity in their femininity and bodily experience.

The muted voice might lend itself to an association with, and reclamation of, feminine sexual difference that the more ascendant voice at times explicitly refuses. According to Bergoffen, then, "the dominant voice of *The Second Sex* urges women to pursue economic independence. The muted voice urges us all to retrieve the erotics of generosity" (36).

Although I agree with Bergoffen that *The Second Sex* "speaks in more than one voice" (1997, 110), I would add that it also speaks in more than two. I do not dispute that there is an opposition in Beauvoir's texts between economic independence and erotic generosity, but there is also a discourse about feminine difference as it is mediated and made possible by the bodily, ethical, and political realms. To this extent I agree with Bergoffen that there is a link between erotic pleasure and political power, but I would pursue their affiliation in a somewhat different direction. Beauvoir makes the connection between power and pleasure in discussing the imbrication of independence and love: "when two partners recognize each other as equals," she writes, "the act of love becomes a free exchange" (Beauvoir 1989, 692). Bergoffen argues on this basis that the erotic can become "the ground of a politics of reciprocity" (1997, 41). Although Bergoffen's conception of the erotic is closely related to the ambiguity of identity (and in particular, that of sexual difference), it also assumes Beauvoir's rejection of the "principle of sacrifice" (132) as well as the idea that Beauvoir's ethical work can provide a "ground" for politics that would then operate on its basis. I am less convinced of both these points. In the first place, the relation of ethics to political power, for Beauvoir, seems to depend not so much upon the renunciation of sacrifice as on its recognition and even acceptance. Moreover, since the subject that Beauvoir theorizes is one whose formation is contingent upon nontotalization, a politics that adheres to any ground other than ambiguity and finitude, even if rooted in the principle of reciprocity, hazards offering absolute identities and principles in which subjectivity might find itself ensnared.

I will argue here that by tracing Beauvoir's positions on equality as they appear on the underside of her writings, we will find that her account of the public sphere, and of the relation between ethics and politics, cannot accommodate any uncomplicated struggle for equal rights, let alone the idea that women must be identified with men in order to be subjects and citizens. In retrieving this aspect of Beauvoir's thought, I hope to realign her with more recent French feminist attempts to elucidate a politics that negotiates feminine difference. I will suggest that there is in Beauvoir a rendering of the universal that is open to the feminine, rather than dismissive of it. In confronting the question of how to reconcile sexual difference with the political necessity for a universal, Beauvoir recognizes that difference, as well as equality, has its relation to the universal.[5] As I will argue, Beauvoir establishes a feminist discursive terrain on which the conflict between equality and difference need not arise. It is not that she presents us with a dialectical synthesis or with the compromise of a "third way," but rather that her work engenders a transformation of concepts, allied with the transformation of the meaning of femininity, that reconceives the relation between equality and difference by moving to a point beyond or prior to their opposition as it is rendered in contemporary feminist discourse. By thinking of these terms in a way that doesn't presuppose their fissure, Beauvoir helps us to find a way out of their apparent conflict that I believe is worth building on. We will find that even her calls for equality in *The Second Sex* neither suppose nor support the liberal recourse to abstract universality. Moreover, understood in this manner, Beauvoir's work forms an historical connection to the writings of other French feminists that enables us to trace a feminist genealogy or inheritance between them. In particular, Beauvoir's provocative suggestion that we think "differences in equality" (1989, 731) anticipates a relation that maintains the tension between difference and equality productively and is also consistent with her theses about the ontological status of subjectivity as nonidentity and ambiguity.

Women's Time, Women's Embodiment

To focus my analysis, I will look briefly at an essay by Kristeva, "Women's Time," and use this as a device to situate Beauvoir's relation to French feminism. In "Women's Time," Kristeva characterizes feminism as emerging in three distinct generations, each with its own specific resolution to the question of women's place within the symbolic contract. By the symbolic contract, Kristeva refers to that process, psychical as well as social, by which the individual takes up, enters, and assumes the position of subject within the domain of law and in a community of others. The symbolic contract implies both the social contract and the field of language as the onset or break of subjectivity. The three generations of feminism, according to Kristeva, thus designate "less a chronology than a *signifying space*, a both corporeal and desiring mental space" (1986, 209). The point of distinguishing among them, therefore, is to delineate the mechanisms by which the desire for justice and identity is deployed, and through which they assume meaning. The first generation, universalist in nature and committed to equality, is best understood as partaking of a "logic of identification" (194); by identifying with "the logical and ontological values of a rationality dominant in the nation-state," this feminism makes political demands on behalf of women while simultaneously rejecting feminine (and maternal) attributes (193–94). The second generation is reactive, responding to the limits and dangers of the first strategy. Whereas the first generation of feminism attempts to reconcile women with the universal through a denial of femininity, the second generation of feminism refuses this assimilationist and difference-negating effort, instead positing women with their own identity and specificity, and attempting to recuperate a notion of feminine difference that is neither repressed nor absorbed by the masculine universal.[6] This latter feminism is, according to Kristeva, less interested in making political demands than in "demanding recognition of an irreducible identity" (194) that is outside the linear time of history. While acknowledging the necessity of this moment, Kristeva is disturbed by its incipient essentialism and worries that such a refusal of history lends itself to a repetition of the patriarchal mythologization of women.

Kristeva points out that the currently ascendant feminism is not one or the other of these first two, but "a mixture of the two attitudes," a feminism that demands both "*insertion* into history and the radical *refusal* of the subjective limitations imposed by this history's time" (1986, 195). In contrast to this state of affairs and its inadequate attempts at reconciliation, Kristeva advocates a third feminism that would move beyond the first two, finding the resources for a feminist generation that would be nonreactive, a feminism that begins with women's desires and bodies but does not attempt to disown the violence and sacrifice that is inherent in the social contract. Violence, according to Kristeva, is an irreducible element of identity because the processes (related both to language and drive) of identity-formation necessitate a subjective splitting and sacrifice. To become a subject is necessarily to suffer a loss, a fissure between law and body. This loss is a violence because it severs bodily pleasure and requires an acceptance of bodily finitude. The break that establishes order also keeps the death drive in permanent play. The third generation of feminism is thus one that will conceive or recognize violence "in the very place where it operates with the maximum intransigence, in other words, in personal and sexual identity" (209), and it will, accordingly, not fall prey to the utopian pretensions of eradicating antagonism from political life.

In particular, Kristeva points to women's desire for motherhood, and to the splitting inherent in pregnancy, as an element that can provide a bodily challenge to identity and that must be accounted for in this new feminism. Because pregnancy is a bodily confrontation with inner alterity, it paradigmatically represents the permanent psychic alterity of the subject and provides a model for relations of otherness and to others. This relation to alterity, however, does not correspond to the "dichotomy man/woman" that Kristeva views as a metaphysical distinction that renders rigid and substantive psychical fluidity and relationality. It is clear therefore that her conception of sexual difference is neither oppositional nor determinate, and that the violence of identity to which she refers is not the violence of sexual rivalry, but the violence within identity and interior to subject-formation, the violence of inescapable aggression necessary to development of a self. It is with reference to this irreducible violence, or sacrifice, that Kristeva calls for a "demassification of the problematic of *difference*" (1986, 209). This is a process that indicates neither reconciliation nor an Hegelian "fight to the death" (ibid.),[7] but rather a localization of difference in the subject's own body and a recognition that bodily characteristics have subjective import and are constitutive of the risks of identity.[8] No subject is one with itself, and the rhythms of the body drive the subject's psychical (dis)order just as language permanently divides us.[9]

At first glance, it seems apparent that Beauvoir is to be classed within the first, universalist, generation of feminism: while the sexed body provides a context, or situation, for identity, Beauvoir seems committed to the existentialist position that the body is the site of immanence and that one's subjectivity is realized in transcendent projects. *The Second Sex,* in particular, seems devoted to the argument that women's bodies have been the prisons of their subjectivity, and that the feminine is a mystification.

Iris Marion Young reads Beauvoir in exactly this way. She claims that Beauvoir is a "humanist feminist" and writes that "humanist feminism consists in a revolt against femininity" defined as "the primary vehicle of women's oppression" (1985, 173). According to Young, Beauvoir believes that "the expectations of femininity which circumscribe the lives of women inhibit the development of their human possibilities" (174), and therefore that equality is to be achieved through the acquisition of masculine identity. Young is, however, wrong about two important points. First, she claims that, as a humanist, Beauvoir finds "gender difference as accidental to humanity" (ibid.), a claim clearly contrary to Beauvoir's attentive and detailed analyses of embodied subjects; we are not accidentally embodied, according to Beauvoir, and therefore surely not accidentally sexed. Beauvoir is not a dualist who assigns identity to mind at the expense of the body. Moreover, while

Beauvoir challenges the myth or mystique of femininity as oppressive, she never confines the terrain of sexual difference to the domain of contingent social construction.[10] As Margaret Simons argues, "Beauvoir's intent . . . is not to deny gender difference as women experience it concretely, but to demystify it" (1999, 163). Becoming a woman, for Beauvoir, is not only an historical event, but a bodily possibility, one that is crucial to full realization of our humanity, even while it also poses a threat given the current shape and meaning of femininity. Second, Young claims that "Beauvoir's humanism identifies the human with men" (1985, 175). This claim also represents a profound misunderstanding. Beauvoir rejects the conflation of masculinity with humanity, even while acknowledging that this conflation has, historically, politically, and linguistically, occurred. When Beauvoir writes in the introduction to *The Second Sex* that "man represents both the positive and the neutral, as is indicated by the common use of *man* to designate human beings in general" (1989, xxvii), she is not identifying the masculine with the human, but criticizing this identification on the part of patriarchal society. The masculine appropriation of subjectivity is not supported but attacked in Beauvoir's text.

Taking precisely the converse position to that of Iris Marion Young, Linda Singer has argued that Beauvoir attempts to reconstitute "femininity as an existential project with an integrity" (1985, 232). Whereas Young's reading locates Beauvoir within Kristeva's depiction of the first generation of feminism, Singer's reading locates her within the second. In Young's terms, Singer reads Beauvoir as a "gynocentric" rather than a "humanist" feminist. Singer contends that the subject's relation to an other might ground Beauvoir's politics, since Beauvoir shifts "the locus of freedom from that of isolated autonomous individuals to freedom emergent from a situation of relatedness and affinity" (ibid.). Singer's assertion is twofold: first, that Beauvoir understands the self as already immersed in caring relations with others; second, that the self, for Beauvoir, is not of the kind that can be regulated or bounded according to law. Taken together, these claims indicate that the subject's bodily finitude is not to be conceived as a coherent border, its subjective status instead permeated temporally, by past and future, and relationally, by others. According to Singer, "being-for-others calls to human freedom as the agency of transformation" (236) that might free "others toward their own possibilities" (238).[11] On this basis, Singer concludes that relatedness itself provides a ground, or a developmental origin, for human freedom. "Beauvoir gives freedom a foundation" (236), she writes, indicating that our relations with others form the fundamental basis of transcendence.

While Singer is right that human finitude, otherness, and difference govern Beauvoir's ethics, it is less convincing that such relationality provides a ground for freedom, or even that such a ground would be desirable. Singer's account of the ground of freedom seems to defy its embeddedness in ambiguity (that is, its groundlessness), replacing it with a secure origin. Our being-with-others is of course a *site* of freedom, but its inherent instability and ambiguity mean it can never securely *ground* our projects; the very instability of these relations is in fact what projects of transcendence allied with human freedom must confront. While Beauvoir's focus on bodily specificity, and on the personal and historical processes by which we become women, supports "a freedom which arises in response to a progressively emergent body in situation" (Singer 1985, 236), we must also be careful to remember that for Beauvoir bodily and social situations are not foundations, but sites (or contexts) through which freedom might be enacted. The subject is without foundations,[12] this being one meaning of ambiguity, of the tension between freedom and nature that is the irresolvable human condition. Beauvoir is closer to Sartre on this point than Singer admits, supporting Sartre's idea of freedom's "groundlessness" insofar as being other to myself also means never finding a secure support for identity and transcendence.[13] As Sartre writes, "[T]he distinguishing characteristic of consciousness . . . is that it is a decompression of being" (1956, 121). What distinguishes consciousness from being-in-itself is the former's noncoincidence with itself, such that "it must necessarily be what it is not and not be what it is" (120). Where the idea of a ground assumes a secure moment of presence or plenitude, consciousness is abandoned precisely because it is not, and cannot be, its own foundation (472). Not only does freedom not have a ground, freedom is not a ground, since it is nothing more than this lack of fixity and coincidence. It is for this very reason that the other, for Sartre, represents a threat to consciousness, posing the danger of capturing me as an in-itself, "paralyzed with facticity" (473).[14]

It therefore seems to me that, contrary to Young's and Singer's misreadings of Beauvoir's project,[15] there is good reason to recognize Beauvoir as on the vanguard of the third generation characterized by Kristeva. Equality politics, with its identitarian demands and refusal to admit difference into the public sphere, cannot acknowledge sacrifice or subjective ambiguity since it supposes that self-present subjects can appear before the law, fundamentally differentiated neither within themselves nor from others.[16] But Beauvior's philosophy of the subject is such that we must recognize her fundamental adherence to the principle of lack both within and between subjects.[17] Beauvoir recognizes a temporal dimension within subjectivity that prevents the self from ever realizing itself as complete, whole, or present to itself. Moreover, the subject for Beauvoir is defined by its finitude and the limits of its bodily nature. There is thus no utopian community in which the separation between subjects might be dissolved or resolved; community entails conflict, division, and negotiation, and as such is itself a risk or project of the subject's possibilities.

Beauvoir's analyses of the independent woman and the mother in *The Second Sex*, and of Sade in "Must We Burn Sade?" as well as her "ethics of ambiguity," all give reason to revise the assumption that Beauvoir is to be situated squarely within the first generation of feminism. In her negotiation of the relations between difference, identity, and equality, Beauvoir clarifies how and why sexual difference cannot be severed from consideration of the most fundamental structures of human experience and the equivocal nature of subjectivity. In her essay on Sade, she confronts and challenges limitless Cartesianism and disinterested Kantianism. And in her development of an ethics, she adopts a complex understanding of the relation of the ethical to the political that is amenable to difference and particularity. In these various aspects of Beauvoir's work, there is evidence that Beauvoir attempts to bridge the universal time of history with the experience of bodily difference, and in so doing to offer a distinctly feminist ethics that addresses the situation of women within the social/sexual contract. If this reading is right, then Beauvoir develops a concept of the subject that is friendlier than one might at first suspect to the risks of identity that Kristeva advocates. It might thus be possible, through an interrogation of Beauvoir's allegiance to equality and universality, to ally her with a feminism, and a subject, oriented by Kristeva's notion of the demassification of difference, especially if we take this to mean that differences cannot be taken as essential oppositions or ossified identitites, but as the dissemination of one's bodily situation into the world, the way in which one's particularity develops in and through mediation of each subject's finite context and relations.

Ambiguity, Finitude, and the Universal

Let us look first at "Must We Burn Sade?" and the problem of abstract universality. Beauvoir praises Sade not for his philosophical or literary accomplishments, but for his moral anxieties and sincerity (Beauvoir 1953, 55). Sade, claims Beauvoir, raises a significant question for the ethical and political subject: "Can we, without renouncing our individuality, satisfy our aspirations to universality?" (12). Because Sade confronts the universal as a social monolith, a set of conventional institutions and the domain of sheerly abstract justice, his answer is no, an answer thus premised upon the meta-physical split by which his own nature is characterized.[18] He views "a world governed by those universal laws which he regarded as abstract, false, and unjust" (25), as liable to consider "men as a mere collection of objects" rather than as "individual beings" (26). His sexual violence, and its concomitant radical individualism, is as much a defiant resistance to the invasion of this universal power to denigrate, as it is an assertion of his own will; in its own way, it expresses a demand for human dignity and freedom. As such, however, it remains commensurate with that against which it defends itself. Sade, in siding against the universal, ends up reinstating it: "as ordered, calculated, and ultimately dispassionate displays of sexual power, they [Sade's excesses] remain within the realm of reason and the economy of exchange" (Bergof-fen 1997, 38). Sade's excesses are excesses of rationality, reason taken to its limit or logical conclusion.

Sade is in many ways too much of a Kantian, trapped by the dictates of abstract reason and the opposition between pleasure and law, and too much a Cartesian, trapped by the conflict "between his consciousness and flesh" (Beauvoir 1953, 42). Unable to accept "the limits of autonomy" (Ber-goffen 1997, 137), Sade responds by living a life of radical solitude. Choosing "to live his subjectivity in the register of the imaginary ego-imago" (123),[19] Sade repudiates the risks of identity inherent in intersubjective relations (and non-egoic intrasubjective ones) in favor of the fantasy of totality. In negotiating the conflicts between universality and individuality, between consciousness and flesh, as well as that between "his social existence and his private pleasures" (Beauvoir 1953, 15), he refuses to suffer the gap between law and particularity. Here we get an inkling of Beauvoir's own response to these conflicts, for although she too is uncomfortable with the gap that sev-ers particularity from the law, she embraces the ambiguity of subjectivity, without recourse to the chimera of complete self-realization.

Beauvoir's answer to the question posed above is, therefore, yes: indi-viduality and universality are indeed equivocally poised, if not resolved, in the subject. It is through the relation to oneself that we come to the universal (which perhaps can find its source in the individual) in a nonabstract way. Sade negotiates the conflict by turning radically toward a morality based on his pleasures because of his "false notions of reciprocity and universality" and the idea of "irreconcilable existences" (Beauvoir 1953, 79), which lead him to detest universal courts of judgment. Although Beauvoir agrees that "Sade's immense merit lies in his taking a stand against these abstractions and alienations" (80), she doesn't confuse the abstract with the universal as Sade does. Without denying the separateness of individuals, Beauvoir articulates the possibility of transcending it, while nonetheless recognizing that "promises of happiness and justice conceal the worst dangers" (82). Beauvoir, in other words, understands separation from others as one aspect of human finitude, but also recognizes the way in which the project of freedom might unite us. She is nonetheless aware that abstract principles can contain and suppress, as well as solicit and support, human freedom, since abstractions can always potentially achieve mastery over self-determination, acting as overriding ideals that hold one hostage by refusing to entertain tension.

Having made an initial foray into the question of the universal, we can now turn to the *Ethics of Ambiguity* to further develop its implications. As we have seen, Beauvoir's attitude toward the universal reveals a complicated view of the relation of the individual to the body politic. She states explicitly that "it is not impersonal universal man who is the source of all values, but the plurality of concrete, particular men" (1994, 17) whose particularity is irreducible. Beauvoir's ethics are decidedly not universalist if this means beginning with a determinate concept of Man under which particular human beings are to be subsumed, and by which their actions are to be judged. It is rather the finite individual to whom Beauvoir grants the privilege of creating value, including the value of the universal. Yet, she also claims that "an ethics of ambiguity will be one which will refuse to deny *a priori* that separate existants can, at the same time, be bound to each other, that their individual freedoms can forge laws valid for all" (18). Such an ethics seems rather to promise, if not guarantee, the possibility of universal law.

Ethics first and foremost establishes a relation to oneself, and the assumption of an ethical relation to oneself is an assumption of one's own ambiguity, as freedom and nature, finite and temporal. This ambiguity, shared by human beings, is the site upon which the possibility for universal law might arise (Beauvoir 1994, 18). The "finite individual" in accepting her or his limits in the "here and now" (121–22) can also be related to others in shared temporality and particularity. The ethical paradox that divides us (from within and from one another) is precisely what we have in common. Thus, although in no way is ethics ontologically prior to living among others, it does seem as though it is the ethical relation that makes possible the political one, insofar as universality emerges from rather than governs finitude. "Society exists only by means of the existence of particular individuals" (122), a claim that carries with it the suggestion that, though universals might come into play, to sediment the social bond and incorporate ethical values, they can never have a prior hold on ethical valuation and judgment. This idea of the universal makes clear that it is not one, as a Platonic Form. Beauvoir insists that she repudiates "all idealisms, mysticisms, etcetera which prefer a Form to man himself" (145). The universal for Beauvoir is not an ideal or mystical entity, but an indicator of the possibility of community that arises from the particularity of human finitude. Universal politics, though it might arise in and through finite individuals, need not establish the atomistic war of the liberal social contract nor "a conflict of opposed wills enclosed in their solitude" (72).[20] Neither must it be the politics of abstract right, in which the individual is lost or subsumed by the demands of formal law. Rather, Beauvoir claims that "the only sure bonds among men are those they create in transcending themselves into another world by means of common projects" (1953, 76). If the political, as Bergoffen writes, "is the domain of the project . . . [and if] it must call upon a 'we'" (1997, 132), this "we" represents the attempt to transcend separateness, and is thus in its own way a realization of freedom in "the risking of the self before the other" (38) and not the self's inversion into certainty. If politics occupies the domain of the universal, it is possible only on the basis of an ethics that is the domain of ambiguity.[21] In establishing an ethical relation to oneself, a relation that sustains rather than denies ambiguity, the possibility is also uncovered for relations with others whose ambiguity is not rendered sterile, abstract, or settled. Conversely, "if we choose to recognize in each subject only the transcendence which unites him concretely with his fellows, we are leading him only to new idols" (Beauvoir 1953, 81), where the agenda of the abstract good will function with indifference or contempt for particularity and finitude.

Because her ethics begins with the particular and reformulates the universal, we must question the assumption that Beauvoir supports a politics of equal rights in any uncomplicated way. When discussing the formal nature of law and the discourse of rights, Beauvoir refers to the attitude of "seriousness." "The serious man," Beauvoir claims, "gets rid of his freedom by claiming to subordinate it to values which would be unconditioned" (1994, 46). Clearly Beauvoir is not denying the political import, perhaps even necessity, of rights; what she does challenge is the way in which rights are invoked as a kind of shield (46, 48) by which one evades one's finitude and responsibility.[22] Rights offer pregiven ends that appear to "emanate from the ethical universe" (48), and thereby they can negate freedom;[23] in appealing to rights, we "dissimulate [our] subjectivity" (ibid.) into the identity of citizenship, a solidified subject purged of ambiguity. Any "objective moralism" that institutes a reification of rights in the political sphere can lead to a suppression of the tension and risks of negativity (133), retreating from rather than embracing ambiguity.

Although ethics is fundamentally about ambiguity, ambiguity is difficult to sustain at the level of politics: "Politics always puts forward Ideas: Nation, Empire, Union, Economy, etc." (Beauvoir 1994, 145), and to this list we might add Citizen, for an idea of the subject of politics is also implicated in its conception. Laws, rights, and universals cannot but solidify values, settling tensions and resolving ambiguity. Yet, if the politics of rights involves bad faith, it would be equally in bad faith to assume that ethical tensions can remain wholly unresolved, that the subject can remain sheerly free and separate; this, as we have seen, was Sade's mistake. There is no pure freedom,[24] divested of bodily finitude or the limits presented by living among others. Evading the Sadean temptation to absolutize freedom, Beauvoir denies that the ambiguity of ethics is subject to the universal cause of freedom (86, 90), and instead inverts the relation. In other words, we must remember that "political choice is an ethical choice" (148) and that ambiguity gives rise to freedom. Politics, though significant, is not for Beauvoir the definitive moment of ethics, and ambiguity cannot be resolved, assimilated, or overcome by political determinations, nor can the tension of ethics be eased through recourse to political absolutes. "Universal, absolute man exists nowhere" (112), Beauvoir declares, and she insists that abstract ethics are commensurately nonexistent. On the plane of the "infinite" (158), abstract universals fail to comprehend the finitude of the subject of ambiguity, grasping only freedom and thereby obviating its tension with nature.

Nonetheless, politics is about power and requires that we remember that "the Other is multiple" (Beauvoir 1994, 144). For this reason, some kind of equality might well be sought as an ethical choice. "Democratic societies," Beauvoir claims, "strive to confirm citizens in the feeling of their individual value" (106). To this extent, the political form of democracy is perhaps better able to sustain the particularity of its finite members than other political structures. If "the rites of justice seek to manifest society's respect for each of its members considered in his particularity" (106–7), then the formation of political rights, and of the universal, might support rather than denigrate an ethical relation of ambiguity. Although this could be read as a classically liberal statement about the rights of citizens and the dignity of man, in this context it more likely suggests the limits of politics and the universal, and points to a dimension excessive to them. Beauvoir indicates a domain of eth-

ics, ambiguity, particularity, and difference that cannot be fully accommo-
dated by political rights or universal laws. Within the ethical domain, freedom is not a metaphysical abstraction, but a possibility entailed by, though
in tension with, embodiment. While liberal equality and rights are premised
upon an ontological conception of the subject as a solitary, autonomous
unit, Beauvoir's equality is premised upon an ontological conception of the
human as finite and dependent on others. The embodied subject is finite,
limited, and sexed.[25]

Maternity and Difference

We can now return to the relation between equality and difference in *The
Second Sex*. As I mentioned earlier, Beauvoir affirms the differences between
men and women: a woman's "relations to her own body, to that of the male,
to the child, will never be identical with those the male bears to his own
body, to that of the female, and to the child" (1989, 731). Notice that difference is here associated with reproduction and sexuality, preeminent aspects
of embodiment and sexual difference. Maternity and sexuality are, moreover,
paradigmatic relations with others. In thinking about this confrontation with
alterity, however, we must remember that, although oriented by the body,
the subject is never simply determined by biological or anatomical givens.
The body to which Beauvoir refers is "not a brute fact" (Beauvoir 1994, 41)
but instead the site of significance and subjectivity, as well as intersubjectivity, insofar as it is through her body that each subject encounters another.
In expressing "our relationship to the world" (ibid.), the body is indispensable to the formation of identity. And bodies, as we know and as Beauvoir
avers, are also the site of difference. Beauvoir's discussion in *The Second Sex*
of women's lives and the concrete situations presented to women by their
embodiment, specifically the experiences of embodied childhood and embodied maternity, also indicates that she is well aware that unconscious iden-
tifications inform both women's identity and the subjective lack implied by
femininity. Power is not only socially wielded, but functions internally as a
force of identification and desire.[26]

Although Beauvoir's writing about motherhood in *The Second Sex* seems
to confine it to immanence and the abandonment of projects of self-determination in the face of an implacable destiny, there is, even within that text,
a countertendency. In making recourse to psychoanalytic categories and
concepts in her chapter entitled "The Mother," Beauvoir also highlights the

ambivalence the mother feels toward pregnancy, childbirth, her husband, and situation. She writes, for instance, that a pregnant woman may be "under the influence of obsessions, fantasies, and memories of infancy that she declines to recognize openly" (1989, 493). Although it is sometimes assumed by her readers that Beauvoir's attitude toward maternity is one that simply dismisses it as an oppressive institution,[27] this is clearly not the case. Motherhood "confronts the mother with the profound human realities of identification and separation" (Simons 1999, 78), and Beauvoir's chapter is devoted to rendering the various attitudes, both complex and conflicted, sometimes loving and nurturing, sometimes hostile and aggressive, that women have toward their situation, and to describing the experience from within women's own point of view. Here as elsewhere her method is to cite first-person sources, and she relies on voices whose experiences together form not a generality but a complicated manifold of particularities. Beauvoir also emphasizes that pregnancy "is experienced in diverse ways according to the relations that exist between the subject and her mother, her husband, and herself" (Beauvoir 1989, 493). Beauvoir's critique of maternity is directed more toward the relation a woman has to the father of her child, and to her own past, and less toward her own relation to the child. In describing the situation or context of patriarchal motherhood, she is attentive to the dangers it presents to women's subjectivity, without being either totalizing or reductive.

Although nowhere does she indicate that pregnancy or maternity in and of itself requires an abdication or mutilation of subjectivity, the perception that Beauvoir views maternity only as a force of patriarchal oppression is perhaps explained by the opening pages of "The Mother." The chapter's first ten pages or so are devoted to an analysis not of mothering but of its prevention, that is, to an analysis of abortion. The illegality of abortion at the time she is writing signifies, according to Beauvoir, a situation in which maternity cannot be freely chosen, and in which women thus lose bodily integrity and independence and are trapped by edicts and laws which withdraw women's agency and inevitably result in the conflation of woman with mother. Against this situation, Beauvoir argues that maternity must take place in a context of choice,[28] that it not be mythologized as an essence or imposed as a destiny,[29] since such a teleological conception is an ethical violation of women's becoming.

Beauvoir is attentive to the social and legal context of pregnancy, childbirth, and maternity because "in the human species nature and artifice are never wholly separated" (Beauvoir 1989, 505). Maternity is not an isolable event or determinate destiny; it is a relation to others that occurs within a socially mediated network of experiences and "it depends upon her relations with her husband, her past, her occupation, herself" (521). Moreover, if the woman is discontent, if her situation denies her independence and self-re-alization, this might also have adverse effects on the child in her care and on their relation. Her rebellion against this situation, or her acquiescence to it, takes form in "symbolic" behavior that is a "grim reality for her child" (513). Here again, Beauvoir shares an insight with psychoanalysis—that an adult's fantasies and anxieties, even (or especially) while unknown to her, will structure the child's universe with signs that it cannot evade. She affirms that "one of the major truths proclaimed by psychoanalysis is the danger to the child that may lie in parents who are themselves 'normal'" (523). Nonetheless, Beauvoir does not abandon the idea that the child might be "an enterprise to which one can validly devote oneself" (522). What she does reject is the postulate that presumes that woman's destiny lies in maternity, that the child "represents a ready-made justification" (522). Like the idea of citizen previ-ously discussed, maternity should not be a pregiven value or ideal to which one sacrifices one's freedom in the misguided belief that transcendence can be realized through devotion to external idols. Beauvoir instead describes it as a "promise" or "engagement" (ibid.); if some of her other descriptions of maternity sound like descriptions of alienation, this is because in their current situation women might well experience alienation from themselves, their bodies, their sexuality, and their children.

The fundamental portrayal of maternity that Beauvoir offers is thus one of the mother's ambivalence. Pregnancy is "a drama that is acted out within the woman herself" (Beauvoir 1989, 495); while a woman's embodiment provides the condition for her individuation, it also provides the possibil-ity for an otherness within her that is the opening for another subjectivity. A pregnant woman's body defies the idea of a self-enclosed ego protected by a clearly demarcated boundary. Instead it offers the scene of a subjective splitting, an alterity that begins in and with the body and an extension of the otherness that is already within each of us. This paradigm of alterity does not simply find oneself (more of the same) in the other, but instead finds the otherness within as a paradigm of the permanent lack of unity that is subjectivity. Beauvoir writes that "in the mother-to-be the antithesis of sub-ject and object ceases to exist," but also that her body is a "striving toward the future" (ibid.). The fetus is both her and not her, it is a "parasite" and she is "no longer anything . . . tossed and driven, the plaything of obscure forces," or she feels it as an "enrichment" and "opulence" (ibid.). Maternity offers an experience of subjectivity and of flesh, of repetition and creation, of transcendence and of invasion. Beauvoir neither extols nor demeans this experience, but reports on its inherent conflicts, all the while avoiding the tendency to mythologize. "Maternity," Beauvoir writes, "is usually a strange mixture of narcissism, altruism, idle daydreaming, sincerity, bad faith, devotion, and cynicism" (513). As with her reading of other myths, Beauvoir is not attempting to uncover a hidden reality lurking behind mystification; rather she recognizes that the maternal myth contains many truths and yet, put another way, that "in this domain there is no truth" (257), no maternal essence. Beauvoir's attentiveness to the details of women's experience of maternity also allies her project to that of Kristeva, since both share the idea that pregnancy is a bodily challenge to identity, while also recognizing that "subjectivity = the ambiguity of the body" (Bergoffen 1995, 191).[30] What is clear for both Kristeva and Beauvoir is that the disunity at the heart of subjectivity (exemplified by pregnancy) might provide an ethical model for the recognition of others in their differences.

Differences in Equality

In contesting the notion of "equality in difference," Beauvoir proposes as an alternative "differences in equality" (Beauvoir 1989, 731).[31] To support a situation in which power is not distributed as relations of dominance does not require of us that we abandon the particularities of identity that mark each of us, and that both give rise to and limit freedom. Where equality in difference tends toward the uniformity of opposition and conflict, differences in equality might tend instead toward the diversity and multiplicity of sexed subjects, toward the demassification of the universal, and its concrete rootedness in finite, and sexed, particularity. Since "particularity is precisely a universal fact" (Beauvoir 1994, 144), the very fact that makes us human and finite, and also that distinguishes and separates us from one another, on its basis we might formulate an ethics both beyond and productive of universal law. There is hence a paradox of particularity: what we share in common is precisely what we don't share with another. For this reason, we can understand that a life with meaning must be a life particularized: a woman recognized only in her social roles as wife and mother is asked to submerge her identity in an abstract category. As Bergoffen writes, "[P]atriarchy coagulates sexual difference into systems of otherness that hide the human being's fundamental ambiguity" (1995, 192).

In attempting to contain differences that might otherwise be disruptive, disputing the fantasy of totality and plenitude, patriarchal structures of sexual difference both neutralize and essentialize the body. Under these auspices, it appears that women must either claim transcendence as neutral instantiations of the universal or as essential incarnations of the Woman. The choice appears to be between equality and difference. But equality doesn't have to be formulated as an equal right to neutral universality or on the basis of an abstract identity of the same. And difference need not be massified as a singular opposition. Differences persist between sexed subjects because identity is rooted in or bonded to bodily morphology, a relation to one's (sexed) capacities. This is why Beauvoir is adamant, in response to the conflict between femininity and subjectivity, that women must take responsibility for reshaping the meaning of femininity, neither abdicating nor exalting it. Bergoffen thus reads Beauvoir as urging us "to accommodate the different ways in which distinctly sexed bodies live their transcendence and ambiguity" (Bergoffen 1997, 170). Since the universal is not for Beauvoir a regulating principle or foundation, its political project need not suppress difference and particularity.

While Young argues that Beauvoir countenances as an ideal for feminists "a universal humanity in which all persons equally realize their potential for self-development" (1985, 180), I would argue to the contrary that for Beauvoir, there is no such thing as a universal humanity apart from our particularity. Her work represents an attempt to develop an ethics not dominated by or governed by universal law. Moreover, insofar as equality might be used to occlude substantive differences, it is not the final word, the absolute value into which subjects must divest themselves. Beauvoir is clearly not demanding an absolute rejection of the universal, but she is suggesting a reorientation of its possibility, forging it through the particular. The universal can thus not function as a foundation or guarantee but is a possibility of the particular, one that resides within the subject's ambiguous relation to itself and others. While the universal is a temptation, it is one whose comforts must be resisted. Beauvoir's ethics are thus beyond universal law—beyond where rights ground and enforce themselves. Moreover, since for Beauvoir transcendence is not a flight from ambiguity but a permanent negotiation with it, equality need not entail the sacrifice of substantive differences.

When therefore Beauvoir calls for equality for women, it is a call for a situation of equal possibilities, for a politics in which each subject's pursuit of her own identity can be unimpaired by political restrictions that impose a pregiven status upon bodily configurations. In "a [political] situation against which all individual action is powerless" (Beauvoir 1989, 724), women are denied the responsibility of their own finitude and rendered prey to passivity and dependence. Equality in this limited political context refers to access to economic agency and the circulation of rights among all citizens; it need not, given Beauvoir's understanding of the ethics of ambiguity, constrain or require women to mimic the subjectivity of men, nor is it a reduction of ethics to the form of the same or of the abstract universal. In this circumscribed political sense, equality can be seen as a redistribution of the concrete possibilities of subjectivity (the possibilities of risk rather than security); engendering this possibility might be both a political and an ethical aim. Thus, although economic and political equality might be necessary points of intervention, this does not exhaust the terrain of practices that might enable women's ambiguous subjectivity to emerge liberated from myth and mystification. In fact, economic independence is clearly insufficient on Beauvoir's terms, since we must also alter the situation in which femininity is mythologized, and which structures women's subjective possibilities.[32] The constitution of the subject is an even more fundamental problem than the relations of dominance in which it finds itself caught.

When Kristeva says of existentialist feminism that it attempts to insert women into the time of project and history, she invokes an account of politics premised upon the demand for equality and the quest for legitimacy grounded in an abstract universal. But if such a notion implies a commitment to universal law and the empty subject, then Beauvoir's account of the ethics of ambiguity, and its subjective priority to relations of power, cannot be situated within its purview. The time of the project is for Beauvoir, not simply the assertion of self-identity, but also the transcendence of separateness in a "we" without pregiven limits, a nonteleological "we" available to subjects whose contours are marked by contingency, particularity, and self-differentiation. This finite "we" can be understood as a demassification of the universal, difference, and the feminine. Though indeed individuated,[33] the individual Beauvoir acclaims is neither a Kantian rational agent nor an atomistic Cartesian, but a subject who cannot be delimited by a fixed identity. Neither entirely self-enclosed nor disinterestedly autonomous, the independence of such a subject is founded not in a settled identity, but rather in the courage to engage with its own constitutive indetermination without forsaking the self-assurance that embodiment offers. Becoming an independent woman thus involves practices that participate in the unsettling of the universal.

NOTES

1. Iris Marion Young advances a similar, and more sustained, critique of Beauvoir in her essay "Humanism, Gynocentrism, and Feminist Politics" (1985). As I will discuss further below, Young articulates two versions of feminism, one humanist, the other gynocentric, and claims that Beauvoir is to be classed as a humanist insofar as she aligns women with a project oriented by individual transcendence.

2. These claims make it clear that Beauvoir does not view femininity as simply an effect of patriarchal relations of domination nor does she understand it as merely mythology or mystification equivalent to an "eternal feminine" or "Platonic essence" (Beauvoir 1989, xxv), as the introduction might suggest. If sexuality marks the intersection of freedom and nature, then femininity is also a condition of human embodiment whose denial is hence dehumanizing. Although the *Second Sex* contributes significantly to the formulation of the sex/gender distinction, Beauvoir's use of the language of femininity does not rigorously distinguish between its multiple meanings (e.g., sex, gender, sexuality, as well as the mystificatory ideals of each of these in the patriarchal imagination).

3. Beauvoir is here more sensitive to the ambiguities of embodiment and alterity than Sartre, whose paradigm of conflict renders both the body and others as a permanent threat to freedom, while also (paradoxically?) making both irrelevant to freedom's ontological status. While Sartre's work is of course not univocal, there is a strong tendency in *Being and Nothingness* to conceptualize freedom in absolute terms, as for instance in the following claims: "there are no *accidents* in a life" (Sartre 1956, 708); "each person is an absolute choice of self" (709); "I *choose* being born" (710).

4. As Beauvoir herself has said, in an interview with Margaret Simons and Jessica Benjamin, "Sartre is a philosopher, and I am not, and I have never really wanted to be a philosopher. . . . I have not created a philosophical work. . . . A philosopher is somebody who truly builds a philosophical system" (Simons and Benjamin 1979, 338). Reading Beauvoir's claim in a generous light, we might say that her rendering of the particular in describing the subjectivity of women is a recreation of philosophy on new terms that escape systematizing gestures, rooting it in finitude and embodiment. If philosophy has posited universals to the exclusion of ambiguity, then Beauvoir gestures toward a new relation between the two.

5. Although my analysis in this essay will primarily be developed with reference to Kristeva, it is worth noting at this point that the idea of a universal aligned with difference rather than unity or plenitude is also one elaborated by Luce Irigaray (who does not consider Beauvoir in this context). In some of her recently translated work (for instance, *Thinking the Difference, I Love to You, Democracy Begins between Two*), Irigaray articulates a conception of the universal as both two and divided, aligned with the division of sex. She refuses the sacrifice of the sensible to the universal (Irigaray 1996, 24) and writes, for instance, that "I belong to the universal in recognizing that I am a woman" (39) and that "the most appropriate content for the universal is sexual difference" (47). In thinking the universal as two, Irigaray thus disrupts the assumption that it must entail oneness or sameness, arguing that these are in fact insufficient to it.

6. It should be noted that, given the way in which Kristeva defines this second movement, she would likely situate Irigaray here.

7. Kristeva thus rejects a notion of recognition predicated on a conflict of forces and directed toward ever more "spiritualized" forms of universality divested of particularity. Her own model of alterity is nondialectical, allowing for the drives to have a permanent relation to the realm of the symbolic without being sublated by it and without presupposing the telos of self-mastery.

8. Identity is risky in part because of the sacrifice and loss that must be undergone, and the vicissitudes of psychic life such sacrifice might entail. There is always the danger of severing what might be necessary and therefore of confronting the return of the repressed or the aggressiveness of the ego. In a more existentialist sense, to assume an identity is also to close off other possibilities.

9. The idea of bodily orientation is related to what Irigaray calls "morphology"— one's orientation to one's self, to others, and to the world; it is premised upon one's embodiment and the limits and possibilities embodiment provides.

10. Such an argument would have to read Beauvoir's claim that "one is not born, but rather becomes, a woman" (Beauvoir 1989, 267) as though the universal human was hidden behind the particular, as though only society particularizes us. Beauvoir's critique of this position will be elaborated below.

11. This transformation of subjectivity that Singer recognizes in Beauvoir is similar to Bergoffen's analysis, which will be discussed below, that situates freedom in a relation to others in which no subject is either essentialized or relegated to inessential status.

12. Singer reminds us, however, of the way in which masculine autonomy has always defined itself as the "overcoming of origins" (1985, 234) or as "freedom without origins" (235). The masculine story of nonorigin clearly is an attempt to suppress the subject's rootedness in bodily finitude and relationality, and therefore is equally, or perhaps more, dangerous than positing a grounding origin, encouraging the masculine flight from ambiguity. Nonetheless, recognizing the maternal body as the situation out of which subjectivity arises does not indicate it provides a foundation.

13. Sartre thus resists the desire to predicate on plenitude or presence what actually emerges from nothingness.

14. This goes a good way toward explaining why Sartre conceptualizes relations with others as conflictual, a struggle between freedoms.

15. In other words, the duality between humanism and gynocentrism that Young develops precisely misses the way in which Beauvoir's project evades this binary, shifting its terms. Moreover, even if we give credence to Young's claim that Beauvoir is a humanist, she is clearly not a liberal universalist, since any universal that is a genuine event of human freedom is not for her premised upon the ground of the atomistic self, but is negotiated out of groundlessness.

16. Moreover, equality politics depends upon the presumption that bodily experience is politically without significance, a thesis patently at odds with Beauvoir's own phenomenology of women's embodiment.

17. Bergoffen discusses this principle of lack in terms of fissure, that human beings are "freedoms who cannot be who they are" (1995, 180).

18. This metaphysical split is both a Cartesian split between consciousness and flesh, self and other, and a Kantian split between pleasure and law.

19. Bergoffen is here relying on the Sartrean rather than Lacanian sense of imaginary, though there are similarities between the two. The imaginary ego-imago is the self reflected back to one as complete, certain, enclosed, and without ambiguity. This self-imago must see itself wholly withdrawn from others in order to avoid any contamination of its identity. Others can therefore make no claim on it, and it is thus in "retreat from the threat of the real" (Bergoffen 1997, 124) of the other's subjectivity.

20. Here we see another important point of agreement between Beauvoir and Kristeva, neither of whom consider the Hegelian dialectic of recognition, premised on conflict and achieved at the expense of the sublation of particularity, to be sufficient for grasping the bonds of community among individuals.

21. This universal is then not a preexisting justification, but a bond negotiated out of negativity and difference.

22. It could be said that rights are the masculine version of what love is for the woman—a means of finding one's identity in an external source to whose transcendence one subordinates oneself. Finding one's purpose outside oneself, whether it be in the ideas of citizen and law, or in love, involves similar processes of bad faith. The chapter entitled "The Woman in Love" in *The Second Sex* appears in the section called "Justifications," and Beauvoir's focus is on those women for whom love is the justification for existence: "So long as she is in love and is loved by and necessary to her loved one, she feels herself wholly justified" (Beauvoir 1989, 653). A woman, Beauvoir claims, will lose herself in another, "transcending her being toward" one who is superior, a man, a subject, identified with and embodying the Law (647), toward "one who possesses all values" (651). And because this love is experienced as a kind of transcendence, such a woman will confuse her commitment and subordination to a man with liberty: "Now, the woman in love is not simply and solely a narcissist identified with her ego; she feels, more than this, a passionate desire to transcend the limitations of self and become infinite, thanks to another who has access to infinite reality. She abandons herself to love first of all to *save herself;* but the paradox of idolatrous love is that in trying to save herself *she denies herself* utterly in the end" (650). The same might be said of the committed citizen. Each effects a displacement of the subject, assimilating her or his identity to another: "the center of the world is no longer the place where she is, but that occupied by her lover. . . . she is another incarnation of her loved one. . . . she is *he*. She lets her own world collapse in contingence, for she really lives in his" (653). Only "when he says 'we'"(ibid.) can the stability and security of her identity be assured. The woman in love believes love will "save her from contingency" (Bergoffen 1997, 199) and, like the good citizen, she is both lost in and united with a subject who is her truth/transcendence.

23. As Jennifer Hansen has noted (unpublished manuscript), the danger in finding one's identity in abstract ideals or concepts is that freedom lies not so much in identification with the value of "liberty" or "equality" as in establishing distance from those values even while retaining commitment to them.

24. Sartre's ideal of sovereignty necessarily entails both unending conflict with others and a notion of absolute freedom, neither of which Beauvoir adheres to.

25. Beauvoir would thus agree with Kristeva that the fantasy of full plenitude is not only an unattainable ideal, but also a dangerous one, more likely to generate aggressivity than curtail it.

26. We can see in these examples that Beauvoir's attitude toward psychoanalysis does not constitute a wholesale rejection. Not only does she praise psychoanalysis for its view of "the body as lived in by the subject" (1989, 38), but she regularly borrows its vocabulary, elaborating concepts like ego, narcissism, identification, and masochism. These concepts are in fact integral to Beauvoir's understanding of the tense relation between being a woman and being a subject.

27. Iris Marion Young is among those who read Beauvoir in this way.

28. Maternity must take place in a context of choice not only for the sake of the health of the mother/child relationship and for the sake of the individual health of each, but also so that women's bodily possibilities will not contradict their capacity for self-determination, that is, precisely so that femininity and subjectivity may cease to be opposed to one another.

29. Her suspicion of the equation between motherhood and womanhood is not unlike Irigaray's in her reading of Diotima's speech (Irigaray 1993b). Both are worried about a formula that establishes a teleology or destiny for women premised on the conflation of femininity with maternity.

30. Kristeva's elaboration of the semiotic dimension of language is consistent with Bergoffen's phrase; bodily drives erupt into language and prevent the closure of the Symbolic, keeping the subject in process.

31. "'Equality in difference,'" according to Beauvoir, is a form of segregation in which the mentality of "'equal but separate'" dominates (1989, xxxv). This formulation supposes that differences are essential attributes of an *other*. Beauvoir declares that "'The eternal feminine' corresponds to 'the black soul' and to 'the Jewish character'" (ibid.), rather than a relation within and between subjects. In other words, this formula conceives of difference as massive or substantive, whereas her reformulation both demassifies difference and allows them to flourish.

32. For this reason, Bergoffen distinguishes between "women's position as the inferior other and woman's status as the inessential other" (1997, 169). "As soon as we see that the standard is sexed" we can also recognize that "movements grounded in demands for equality lead to dead ends" (ibid.). Moreover, "by refusing to equate women's liberation from the status of the inessential other with woman's entry into the domain of the patriarchal subject, Beauvoir indicates that the transformation of patriarchy requires a transformation of the concept of the subject" (ibid.).

33. "Is this kind of ethic individualistic or not?" Beauvoir asks. "Yes," she answers, "but it is not solipsistic" (1994, 156). With this distinction, she indicates that freedom is "achieved only through the freedom of others" (ibid.), a position which clearly resists any atomistic conception of the individual. Bergoffen notes that "we begin with our differences from each other. The ethical question concerns the ways in which we negotiate these differences" (Bergoffen 1997, 174).

REFERENCES

Beauvoir, Simone de. 1953. "Must We Burn Sade?" In *The Marquis de Sade: An Essay by Simone de Beauvoir, with Selections from His Writings Chosen by Paul Dinnage*. New York: Grove Press. 9–82.

———. 1989. *The Second Sex*. New York: Vintage.

———. 1994. *The Ethics of Ambiguity*. New York: Citadel.

Bergoffen, Debra. 1995. "Out from Under: Beauvoir's Philosophy of the Erotic." In *Feminist Interpretations of Simone de Beauvoir*. Ed. Margaret A. Simons. University Park: Pennsylvania State University Press. 179–92.

———. 1997. *The Philosophy of Simone de Beauvoir: Gendered Phenomenologies, Erotic Generosities*. Albany: State University of New York Press.

Irigaray, Luce. 1993a. *Je, Tu, Nous: Toward a Culture of Difference*. New York: Routledge.

———. 1993b. "Sorcerer Love." In *An Ethics of Sexual Difference*. Ithaca: Cornell University Press. 20–33.

———. 1994. *Thinking the Difference*. New York: Routledge.

———. 1996. *I Love to You*. New York: Routledge.

———. 2001. *Democracy Begins between Two*. New York: Routledge.

Kristeva, Julia. 1986. "Women's Time." In *The Kristeva Reader*. Ed. Toril Moi. New York: Columbia University Press. 188–213.

Sartre, Jean-Paul. 1956. *Being and Nothingness*. New York: Washington Square Press.

Simons, Margaret A. 1999. *Beauvoir and The Second Sex: Feminism, Race, and the Origins of Existentialism*. Lanham, Md.: Rowman and Littlefield.

Simons, Margaret A., and Jessica Benjamin. 1979. "Simone de Beauvoir: An Interview." *Feminist Studies* 5, no. 2:330–45.

Singer, Linda. 1985. "Interpretation and Retrieval: Rereading Beauvoir." *Women's Studies International Forum* 8, no. 3: 231–38.

Young, Iris Marion. 1985. "Humanism, Gynocentrism and Feminist Politics." *Women's Studies International Forum* 8, no. 3: 173–83.

3   Reading Beauvoir with and against Foucault

SONIA KRUKS

THE BEST OF WHAT "postmodern feminism" has so far developed is a series of radical glosses on Simone de Beauvoir's now classic starting point: "one is not born a woman: one becomes one."[1] For, like the work of Beauvoir, postmodern approaches enable us to de-essentialize and de-naturalize the concept of "woman." In particular, creative appropriations of Foucault's genealogical methods have enabled feminist scholars to explore the ways in which representations of "woman" have shifted over time. Foucault's insights into the inseparability of power and knowledge, and his explorations of the disciplinary practices that produce "subjectified" subjects, have also made his methods a valuable resource for a wide range of feminist analyses of women's subordination.

But there are also difficulties for feminism—and other emancipatory movements—in appropriating Foucault too fully or too uncritically. In reading Foucault both through and against Beauvoir in this essay, I seek to illuminate and address some of these difficulties. By pointing not only to the divergences but also to the striking complementarities between the two thinkers, I aim to challenge views of Beauvoir and Foucault as advocates, respectively, of "Enlightenment" and "post-Enlightenment" philosophies that are starkly antithetical. For the binary oppositions between Enlightenment and post-Enlightenment thought, between modernity and postmodernity, that too many protagonists on either "side" of recent debates have accepted, are themselves highly problematic.

More specifically, I argue that Foucault's insightful account of the production of "subjectified" subjects is, as it stands, still inadequate, especially for feminist politics. It either remains at the level of description or else, at an explanatory level, falls into a problematic functionalism, which unreflectively attributes an inherent and teleological rationality to subjectifying practices. In reading Foucault through the lenses of Beauvoir we can find means more adequately to explain what Foucault describes. I also argue that reading Foucault through Beauvoir enables us to reintroduce into his analyses notions of personal agency and moral accountability that remain important for any project of emancipatory politics. Foucault claims to deny the importance of such notions, yet his work still tacitly presupposes them. Beauvoir's concern with the ethical aspects of subjectification can be used to bring both greater intellectual coherence and explicit moral import to Foucault's work.

Foucault's work is, of course, far from monolithic. In what follows I am concerned with the Foucault of the mid-1970s; that is, a Foucault whose focus is less on the "care" of the self than on the anatomo-political production of the self. For this is a Foucault with whom feminist theory has pervasively engaged: the Foucault of *Discipline and Punish* (French 1975), the first volume of *The History of Sexuality* (French 1976), and the essays published in English in *Power/Knowledge* (1980); this is a thinker whose focus is on the inseparability of power and knowledge, and on their constitutive role in the production of the subjectified subject through disciplinary and normalizing practices. This is a Foucault for whom subjectivity is so thoroughly produced "from the outside in" (Grosz 1994), by the micro-practices of power, that to ask questions about the degree to which freedom or moral capacity might be attributes of subjecthood appears simply irrelevant.

It is also the Foucault whose work has a distinctly functionalist, even a teleological, cast insofar as disciplinary practices are said to take on purposive attributes that have traditionally been ascribed to the individuated human subject. Discipline is frequently personified or anthropomorphized. It knows what it is doing; it acts in an intentional, goal-oriented, rational manner, to perform necessary social functions. For example, Foucault writes: "discipline *had to solve* a number of problems for which the old economy of power was not equipped. . . . *it arrests or regulates* movements; *it clears up* confusion. . . . *It must also master* all forces that are formed from the very constitution of an organized multiplicity; *it must neutralize* the effects of counter-power that spring from them and which form a resistance to the power that wishes to dominate it" (1977a, 219; emphases added).

This is not to deny that one can still find reflections on freedom in Foucault's work; but freedom is not an attribute of the subject, or of individual agents. Rather, freedom is cast as the "insurrection" of subjugated knowledges

(Foucault 1980, 84), or as the emergence of "transgressive" discourse that has purpose of its own; transgression too has agency, but no specific authors. One might talk not only of a history without a subject, or of a text without a subject, but also of agency and freedom without a subject. As with discipline, Foucault personifies transgression, attributing to it intentional agency, rather than attributing such agency to persons. He writes, for example, that "transgression does not seek to oppose one thing to another. . . . its role is to measure the excessive distance that it opens at the heart of the limit and to trace the flashing line that causes the limit to arise" (1977b, 35).[2]

What difference does it make who is speaking? In his essay "What Is an Author?" Foucault suggests that the notion of individual authorship emerged at a particular moment in the history of ideas, a moment when "individualization" came to be privileged. That moment, he argues, has now passed: "it is a matter of depriving the subject (or its substitute) of its role as originator, and of analyzing the subject as a variable and complex function of discourse" ([1979] 1984, 118). The issue of authorship, then, is part of a wider set of debates about the status of "the subject," about whether human actors are knowing and volitional subjects, and about freedom. But above all, for Foucault, "the subject" in question is the subject of French phenomenology. Thus, for example, in a 1977 interview he stated:

> I don't believe the problem can be resolved by historicizing the subject, as posited by the phenomenologists, fabricating a subject that evolves through the course of history. One has to dispense with the constituent subject, to get rid of the subject itself, that's to say, to arrive at an analysis which can account for the constitution of the subject within a historical framework. . . . genealogy . . . is a form of history which can account for the constitution of knowledges, discourses, domains of objects etc., without having to make reference to a subject which is either transcendental in relation to the field of events or runs in its empty sameness throughout the course of history. (1980, 117)[3]

This statement opposes stark alternatives: on the one hand a conception of the subject as "constituent" (or constituting) and as "transcendental" to history, that is, unsituated; on the other a conception of the subject as constituted and to be analyzed (through genealogy) as no more than an "effect" of its historical framework. In it we find posed those dualities, between humanism and antihumanism, between "Enlightenment" and "postmodernity," that we need to put into question. For in order to account (with Foucault) for the weight of social structures, discourses, and practices in the formation

of the subject, and yet still to acknowledge (against Foucault) that element
of freedom which enables us also to consider the self as a particular and intentional agent that remains responsible for what it does, we need a far more
complex account of the subject than Foucault would appear to grant us.[4]

It is with this in mind that I return to Beauvoir and read Foucault and
Beauvoir through and against each other. Much of Beauvoir's painstaking
and detailed account in *The Second Sex* of the young girl's *formation* and the
perpetuation of "femininity" could be retold in the Foucauldean modes of
"the political technology of the body," of "discipline," of "normalization,"
and of "panopticism."[5] Yet she still adheres to a notion of the *repression* of
freedom that Foucault would not endorse. However suppressed, however
"disciplined," it is still freedom-made-immanent that distinguishes even the
most constituted human subject from a trained animal. A real repression—
or oppression—of the self is always possible for Beauvoir. For Foucault—at
least as he expressly presents his position—this is not the case.

I will pursue this divergence primarily through the notion of "panopticism," of the place of the gaze or look in producing docility, as Foucault
and Beauvoir respectively treat it. For Beauvoir, "becoming a woman" also
involves subjectification through what Foucault will call panoptic practices.
But to understand this process of "becoming" we must also explore the ways
in which subjectification is lived and taken up by the subject, be it in modes
of complicity, of resistance, or both. This "lived" aspect of subjectification
cannot be accessed through Foucault's explicit framework of analysis, yet,
I suggest, his own analyses actually require that we acknowledge and consider it.

Panopticism is, according to Foucault, the quintessential form of the
method of "hierarchical observation" that is integral to much disciplinary
power. It is a mechanism "in which the techniques that make it possible to
see induce effects of power" (1977a, 170–71). It is a crucial (though certainly
not the sole) component of those modern disciplinary practices that produce
the normalized subject, both in formal disciplinary institutions and beyond.
In Bentham's ideal prison, in which each isolated inmate lives—and *knows*
himself to live—under continual inspection from the all-seeing (but anonymous) eye of the guard, the major effect of the Panopticon is "to induce
in the inmate a state of conscious and permanent visibility that assures the
automatic functioning of power" (210). Interiorizing the scrutinizing gaze
to which he (or she) is subjected, the inmate becomes effectively (and effi-
ciently) self-policing: "He who is subjected to a field of visibility, and who
knows it, assumes responsibility for the constraints of power; he makes them

play spontaneously upon himself; he inscribes in himself the power relation in which he simultaneously plays both roles; he becomes the principle of his own subjection" (202–3).

Panopticism is not confined to particular institutions, such as the prison or the asylum. On the contrary, Foucault conceives it to be a general "modality of power" in normalizing societies such as ours. Moreover, women are subject to (and subjects of) what Foucault refers to as "the minute disciplines, the panopticisms of everyday" (1977a, 223), in a particularly all-encompassing and complex manner that he does not himself explore. Indeed, Beauvoir's account of how one "becomes a woman" intriguingly anticipates Foucault's later account of panopticism. As she describes it, becoming a woman requires developing an awareness of one's "permanent visibility," learning continually to view oneself through the eyes of the generalized (male) inspecting gaze and, in so doing, taking up as one's own project those "constraints of power" that femininity entails. But becoming a woman is, for Beauvoir, still an intentional process, even though it is enacted within the constraints of power. Thus questions that Foucault leaves hanging in midair, concerning *how* this modality of power functions, are more adequately addressed by Beauvoir.

Foucault is sometimes a slippery thinker. His previously cited claim, that we need "to get rid of the subject itself," and his affirmations that the subject comes into being as simply the effect of power, are tacitly put into question by passages such as the one I just quoted from *Discipline and Punish*. Such passages imply something else: an active, even, one could argue, a quasi-constituting, subject; a conscious subject who "knows" that he is visible; one who "assumes responsibility" for the effects of power on himself, and who is active in playing "both roles," that of scrutinizer and scrutinized. But just how and why does the panoptic gaze induce such an active compliance? It is not clear. "Just a gaze," Foucault says. "An inspecting gaze which each individual under its weight will end by interiorizing to the point that he is his own overseer, each individual exercising this surveillance over, and against, himself" (1980, 155). But how and why does an individual interiorize the gaze? What kind of subjectivity is capable of such an interiorization? Or—most important—of resisting it? For, as Foucault acknowledges, there has also been "effective resistance" to various forms of panoptic scrutiny (162).

But while Foucault's own analyses actually call for an account of the subject as both constituted and constituting, as playing "both roles," he does not acknowledge this, perhaps because of his concern to distance himself from his phenomenological fathers. Thus his explicit pronouncements, that "the subject" is produced through panoptic and other disciplinary "subjectifying" practices, and the implicit presuppositions of his account come to be at odds with each other. Foucault claims that "power relations can materially penetrate the body in depth, without depending even on the mediation of the subject's own representations. If power takes hold of the body, this isn't through its having first to be interiorised in people's consciousnesses" (1980, 186). Yet, we have seen, panoptic power *does* have to be interiorized in a way that engages consciousness; and if its interiorization can be resisted this implies also that, in some manner and to some degree, individuals may choose how to respond to it. Resistance cannot be explained solely as the result of the self-functioning of transgressive discourses, or of the deployment of subjugated knowledges (though it might be incited or invited by these). On the contrary, it also involves individual responses that imply some play of intentional consciousness, even of what we might call freedom.

Foucault reverses traditional forms of mind-body dualism by privileging the body as the site of the formation of the self, yet he is still caught up in this dualism. If the interiorization of power takes place through "the body," then it can of course bypass that—allegedly—distinct entity called "consciousness." But if, with Beauvoir (who here draws on Merleau-Ponty), we insist that the body is *not* distinct from consciousness but rather is the *site* of their interconstituency, and the site of a sentient and intentional relation to the world, then the modalities through which we interiorize and/or resist the panoptic gaze can be explored more adequately.

Judith Butler has suggested that there are ways in which "the body" comes to be a substitute—and an inadequate one at that—for the psyche in Foucault's theories (Butler 1997, 94). She rightly argues that Foucault leaves us with the problem of how to understand "not merely the disciplinary production of the subject, but the disciplinary cultivation of *an attachment to subjection*" in the modern self (102). Butler turns to a psychoanalytic framework to address this problem, but in what follows I offer an alternate route. I return to Beauvoir and to her phenomenological explorations of the look, or gaze, in order to examine further some of the issues of complicity and resistance to power that Foucault implicitly raises.

In Foucault's general discussions of power—of power as capillary and circulating—normalization proceeds through panoptical and other disciplinary practices in which, as subjectified subjects, as both the effects of power and the bearers of power, we are all implicated. As he puts it, "power is employed and exercised through a netlike organization. And not only do individuals circulate between its threads; they are always in the position of simultaneously undergoing and exercising power. . . . The individual . . . is not the *vis-à-vis* of power; it is I believe, one of its prime effects" (1980, 98). However, in discussing the generalized masculine gaze, under and through which women become and remain women, Beauvoir suggests that men and women are not subjected to the same forms of power, nor subjected to power to the same degree. At one level Beauvoir agrees with Foucault: the generalized power of men over women is possessed by no specific individual. Thus, she points out, an individual man who wishes to cease participating in the privileges of masculine power finds that he cannot withdraw from it; it is not his to renounce. "It is useless to apportion blame and excuse. . . . a man could not prevent himself from being a man. So there he is, guilty in spite of himself and burdened by this fault he did not himself commit" ([1949] 1989, 723).

Even so, men and women, as socially distinct groups, are differently positioned within generalized networks of power in ways that Foucault does not recognize. Furthermore, as Beauvoir sees very clearly, their differential positionings may easily permit the actual "possession" of power by a particular man over a particular woman. In Beauvoir's France the marriage contract still brought into being a form of "sovereign" power, in which a husband unambiguously controlled his wife's finances, domicile, access to her children, and so on. Beauvoir was acutely aware of the significance of what we might call the institutional dimensions of masculine power, as they mutually enabled and reinforced those more diffuse forms of power that Foucault describes as disciplinary or normalizing. For it was not the case that "power [was] no longer substantially identified with an individual who possesses or exercises it by right of birth" (Foucault 1980, 156). On the contrary, in marriage, right of birth alone still conferred juridical grants of "sovereign" power to husbands in Beauvoir's world. Although such power does not formally exist today, at least in most Western liberal democracies, the institutional dimensions of continuing masculine privilege should not be underestimated.

If we are to understand women's complicity in sustaining those normalizing practices through which their subordinating "femininity" is perpetuated, we will need also to look at juridical, economic, and other institutional arrangements in which women find themselves located. These often still produce de facto relationships of personal privilege and dependency that make compliance a rational survival strategy for many women.[6] We will need also to look at the ways in which women become invested in their femininity, not only as a material survival strategy but as a mode of lived experience that is integral to the self. It is in exploring the less calculating ways in which women become invested in their femininity that Beauvoir allows us to examine also "from the inside out" (Grosz 1994) Foucault's account of the disciplinarily constituted subject. When discussing the Panopticon, Foucault writes, "[W]e are talking of two things here: the gaze and interiorisation" (1980, 154). However, he does not ever explain how the latter, the interiorization of the gaze, is effected. Nor does he show how it brings into being the complicity of the self-surveilling subject; nor (more generally) does he reveal how the continuous and minute disciplining of the body that he describes produces its correlative "soul."

It is, on reflection, quite remarkable that in the three hundred or so pages of *Discipline and Punish* we get absolutely no sense of what it *feels* like to be subjected to the panoptical gaze; nor are we given any sense of the experiential dimension of becoming a self-surveilling "subject" of panopticism.[7] Foucault's disciplinary subjects do not appear to feel fear, anxiety, frustration, unhappiness. Such emotions, not to mention pain, are strikingly absent from his account. It is here that Beauvoir's analysis adds another necessary dimension to Foucault's. We do not need to posit a Cartesian knowing subject or a pure constituting consciousness to understand *how* the practices of power are taken up, or interiorized, by an individual self or "soul"—that may inflect, deflect, accept, or resist them in multiple and idiosyncratic ways. However, we do need to posit a subject that is active and intentional to some degree. Beauvoir's account of an embodied and situated subject—a subject that, while never being an absolute freedom or pure consciousness, has a viewpoint on the world and an intentional relationship with it—offers us what Foucault lacks.

Beauvoir's account of women's diverse interiorizations of the male gaze involves a creative reworking of Sartre's phenomenology of "the look" in *Being and Nothingness.* For Sartre, another's look is always experienced as a threat. For to be seen by another is to become an object in his world; and to be aware of myself as being seen by another is to be aware of myself as object-like. The look is thus always experienced as an assault on my freedom; it assails my ability to define for myself the meaning of my situation.[8] However, for Sartre, I am always free to reaffirm my status as a subject by turning the tables on the Other, by in turn looking at him.

I have argued elsewhere (Kruks 1990, 83–112) that Beauvoir radically modifies Sartre's account of self–other relations by insisting that, where there are relations of social equality, objectification can be superseded by forms of mutually validating "reciprocity" (Beauvoir [1949] 1989, xxiii). The look can be a means of expressing friendship or love, of sharing, of validating another; it can, in short, be intersubjective, rather than objectifying. However, in those formal institutions that Foucault characterizes as panoptical—the prison, the asylum, the school, the army parade-ground, and so on—sur-veillor and surveilled are not equally positioned, and the look thus functions irreversibly to objectify. Indeed, in Bentham's design for the Panopticon it is essential that the inmates are illuminated and visible to the inspecting gaze of the guard or overseer, but that he is not equally visible to them. Similarly, those assembled for inspection, such as soldiers on the parade ground, may not look back at those who inspect them.

To be subjected to a gaze that one cannot reciprocally return is, indeed, to experience objectification, or an alienation of one's subjectivity. I experience a loss of my immediate, lived subjecthood as I become fixed or immobilized *in my own eyes* as the object that I am (or believe myself to be) in the eyes of the one who looks at me. However, this experience is not *by itself* sufficient to account for the production of docility and of compliant self-surveillance that Foucault attributes to the power of the panoptic gaze.

What is also essential here is what Sartre and Beauvoir call "shame": a relation to oneself, in the presence of another, in which one *evaluates* one-self negatively through the look of the other. Sartre begins his discussion of shame in *Being and Nothingness* with the well-known example of hearing somebody else approaching while, "moved by jealously, curiosity, or vice," I am peeping through a keyhole ([1943] 1956, 259). The experience of shame in being "caught" in such a circumstance involves not only seeing myself as the object that the other sees, but seeing myself as the other will *judge* me: as reprehensible, faulty, inferior. Moreover, I do not just feel shame of my act, but of my *self*. For suddenly I *am* as I am seen to be: "shame . . . is shame of *self*; it is the *recognition* of the fact that I *am* indeed that object which the Other is looking at and judging" (261). Here, we have an initial account of how the power-effect of the look, which Foucault only observes, actually operates. We see how, in interiorizing the shaming look, I become not only the object of my own surveillance but also the judge of myself.

But Sartre's account of shame calls out for further elaboration—which Beauvoir offers in her descriptions of feminine experience. First, I can come to feel shame by virtue of such facticities as my bodily characteristics or my social status without having engaged in any specific act. I may judge myself to be ugly, for example, if my body does not conform to the norms of beauty in my society. Or, if I am a member of a class of people, such as women, that is deemed to be socially inferior, I may judge myself to be inferior.[9] Second, although I may come to judge myself through the look of a single individual, as in Sartre's example, I may also do so through an impersonal or anonymous, an entirely nonspecific, or even in the long run absent, Other. In the panoptical institutions that Foucault describes, the look is impersonal but presumed present: continuous scrutiny on the part of designated officials is part of the disciplinary regime. But in other instances, the look is generalized or nonspecific; "they," "others," "society," judge certain of my characteristics to be signs of my inferiority. And, in its most strongly interiorized forms, the look may become so integral to the self that it functions in a situation of total privacy—as when a woman carefully applies her makeup even if she intends to stay at home on her own the whole day and will be "seen" by ab-solutely nobody but herself. In these latter cases we might appear to return to notions of panoptical power as circulating and capillary, to Foucault's "minute disciplines, the panopticisms of everyday," in which nobody pos-sesses power. Yet, when we come to look more closely, contra Foucault and as Beauvoir realizes, some are more disciplined, more normalized, and less powerful than others—among them, women.

Woman, as Beauvoir depicts her, is not just man's Other, she is his *inferior* Other: "The relation of the two sexes is not like that of two electrical poles, for man represents both the positive and the neutral, so that in French [as in English] one says "men" to designate human beings. . . . He is the Subject, he is the Absolute—she is the Other" ([1949] 1989, xxi). Whereas Sartre argues that by returning the look one can always turn the tables on the Other, Beau-voir suggests that what distinguishes the situation of woman is precisely her *inability* to do so. "No subject," she observes, "immediately and voluntarily affirms itself as the inessential"; thus the question is "from whence comes this submission in women?" (xxiv).

In answering this question Beauvoir offers us a series of descriptions of how women come to exist in the mode of inferiority and to subsume it into forms of subjectified feminine subjectivity. If "not every female human being is necessarily a woman" ([1949] 1989, xix), then we need to grasp the processes through which "one becomes one" as not only the exercise of power upon and its transmission through the subject, but also as it is interiorized, taken up, and lived. It is here that the panopticisms of daily life and the "interior" experiences of shame they induce are crucial.

Beauvoir begins by describing the multitude of small disciplines to which female children are often subjected and which still today induce passivity, timidity, and physical self-constraint.[10] But she suggests that it is at puberty that more profound experiences of shame usually begin. At that time, a girl often becomes the object of stares, whistles, derogatory remarks on the street (and at school in coeducational systems) and, simultaneously, is required to hide from view the newly acquired "secret" of menstruation. In the experience of menstruation (at least in Western society) a young woman's profound sense of herself as not only the Other but as the inferior Other is dramatically discovered. She must ensure that she does not appear soiled in public; must learn discreetly to dispose of bloodied pads, tampons, and clothing; is warned that she might give away her "condition" by the smell of menstrual blood should she not keep herself sufficiently clean.[11]

In such ways, a young woman learns how to develop those practices of self-surveillance and self-discipline that Foucault attributes to the panoptic gaze. But they are not the *direct* effect of the gaze itself, so much as of the shame with which it forces her to see "herself." Shame, as what we might call a primary structure of a woman's lived experience, extends far beyond her relationship to menstruation, and it becomes integral to a generalized sense of inferiority of the feminine body-subject. A woman, Beauvoir writes, "*is* her body; but her body is something other than herself" ([1949] 1989, 29).

As Beauvoir's account of women's lived experience proceeds, from early childhood, through girlhood, sexual initiation, marriage, childbirth, and motherhood, toward old age, shame remains a primary structure of experience. Shame of an embodied self that is always marked as inferior, as defective, is instrumental to women's participation in the multitude of minute daily practices that induce docility and reproduce forms of normalized feminine behavior.[12] Nor does the woman who resists, the would-be "independent" woman whom Beauvoir describes in the final section of *The Second Sex*, escape from it.

On the contrary, Beauvoir points out, the would-be independent woman lives her femininity as a painful contradiction. Brought up (as most girls still are today) to see herself through the male gaze, enjoined to passivity, and to make herself desirable to man, she *is* her femininity. Her being-for-others is profoundly gendered. This is not a facticity that can be ignored, since it thoroughly permeates her being-for-herself. She cannot renounce her femininity, for it is constitutive of her selfhood even as it undercuts her struggle for self-affirmation. The "independent" woman thus lives divided against herself even more starkly than the woman who more fully accepts traditional feminine roles.[13]

Moreover, because Woman is not merely man's Other but an inferior Other, Beauvoir is keenly aware that individual solutions are not fully realizable. This is not to say that individual women should cease to mount a personal challenge to normalizing femininity. But in challenging it they will disclose the radical inequality of their situation and encounter the limits to what can be individually achieved. Beauvoir is far from affirming the untrammeled capacity for freedom, or "transcendence," of which she is often accused. On the contrary, she would agree with Foucault that it is through subjection to disciplinary and normalizing practices that subjectivity comes into being. The feminine subject cannot simply shed her femininity, for there is no "inner" subject that can, in absolute freedom, transcend its body and its situation; there is no pure constituting consciousness. But to acknowledge this is not to deny all freedom to the subject. For most women, a range of choices is still open as to *how* one interiorizes, assumes, and lives normalized femininity. Thus, issues of personal agency, ethics, and responsibility, which cannot consistently be posed within Foucault's explicit framework, emerge as central for Beauvoir.

Beauvoir posits a continuum of situations. At one end of the continuum, she offers an account of the subject that could be recast in Foucault's starkest terms. She talks of the woman who lives in a situation of such extreme subjection that freedom is made immanent, is no more than a suppressed potentiality. Here a woman *is* so thoroughly her situation, so thoroughly its product, that no effective choice as to how it is to be lived is possible. Such a woman is, as Foucault had put it, a constitut*ed,* not a constitut*ing* subject (1980, 117).

But while immanence marks one end of a continuum of theoretically possible situations, it is doubtful if many women actually live in such a condition. At the other end of the continuum is the "independent" woman, who struggles doggedly against the constraints of her situation and in so doing reveals the impossibility of fully transcending it. Most women, however, live neither in total immanence nor in a mode of continuous revolt. They live somewhere between, embracing various modes of complicity, compromise, or resistance, each of which has both rewards and costs attached to it. Here we return, with Beauvoir, to those issues of complicity with subjection, and to those questions of individual resistance that Foucault's account of subjectification tacitly poses but does not adequately address.

Near the end of *The Second Sex* Beauvoir observes that men find in women "more complicity than the oppressor usually finds in the oppressed" ([1949] 1989, 721). The term "complicity" for Beauvoir connotes a moral register, absent in Foucault's account of the subject's "compliance" in disciplinary power. What both Beauvoir and Foucault share is the insight that the subject of disciplinary power actively participates in it: power is not unidirectional, nor simply top-down. We have already seen that Beauvoir accounts more fully than Foucault for *how,* through self-objectification and shame, disciplinary power is internalized so that its subject comes also to be its agent. But, beyond the "how," there are also questions of "why." Beauvoir also suggests that in many instances complicity could be more fully resisted. The subjectified subject, which takes up those practices of power through which it is both constituted and self-constituting, still enjoys a degree of freedom as to how it assumes them. Here, ethical issues begin to arise; for if the subject enjoys a degree of freedom, complicity is not just a fact to be described but a choice, a project, that is open to moral evaluation. It is a matter of what, following Sartre, Beauvoir will call "bad faith," "flight," or the choice of "inauthenticity."

After decades of popular self-help manuals, the term "authenticity" often connotes today a highly psychologized notion of the search for "inner meaning" or the quest to get in contact with one's "real self." But for Beauvoir—as for Foucault—there is no real or inner self "there" to be discovered. Rather, what is at issue here is the choice of an ethical stance in the face of one's situation and its facticities. In inauthenticity, a woman affirms her selfhood to be constituted by exterior conditions and forces even when this is not wholly the case. The "bad faith," or self-deception, lies in the fact that one is still making choices and exercising a degree of freedom, while claiming to be unable to do so. Very rare circumstances apart, one is not free not to choose how one takes up one's situation. To "become a woman" is not to be sculpted by exterior forces like a lump of clay. To claim an analogously inert status, to claim that one is "constituted" through and through, is in bad faith to flee one's freedom.[14] Beauvoir thus insists that, however constrained our situation, we can almost always still take it up in different ways, and that we must accept responsibility for our own choices and values.

Today, few Western women fit the details of Beauvoir's outdated portrait of the inauthentic housewife in *The Second Sex*. Yet surprisingly many of her insights remain pertinent. Self-abnegation and denial; deference to the opinions of others and failure to assert one's own; limiting one's goals and ambitions, particularly to fit in with those of a lover or husband or child: all of these typically "feminine" forms of behavior still endure among a diverse range of women today. They can, of course, often be explained as rational, even self-interested, strategies on the part of those who are still, to a significant degree, economically dependent on men. In a Foucauldean vein, one can also account for them as strictly the effects of those disciplinary and normalizing practices through which women are constituted as subjects. But if neither explanation is wrong, neither is by itself adequate. For "feminine" behavior is more than either a calculated strategy or a discursively produced effect. It is more than a strategy because being a woman is not an identity that an "inner" self could pick up or shed at will. It is more than a discursive effect because it is interiorized and taken up in ways that are both constrained and yet still indeterminate, and open to moral evaluation.

It is from this indeterminacy that feminism, as a political project, begins. It must acknowledge the margin of freedom that enables us to struggle against our complicity in subordinating and subjectifying practices—as well, of course, as to struggle against the institutional dimensions of subordination, such as legal lack of control over our own bodies, or unequal pay. Feminism should not be shy to affirm its values, for any emancipatory project implies an ethical stance. And, indeed, as Beauvoir argues, given even the smallest margin of freedom, we cannot avoid affirming values in all that we do. To deny this is to act in bad faith and lay claim to an irresponsibility we do not enjoy.

It is also true, of course, that no emancipatory project is entirely innocent. As Foucault has so clearly pointed out, all claims to truth, or affirmations of values, are also productive of power effects. However, this does not mean that we should endeavor not to affirm our own values lest, in the name of truth, we become yet further complicit with power.[15] The better safeguard, as we learn from Beauvoir, is to make explicit the values implied by our actions, while also recognizing our responsibility for the power effects they produce.

NOTES

1. I use the term "postmodern feminism" somewhat reluctantly since it can cover such a diversity of positions. However, it does connote an intellectual style and a cluster of loosely shared assumptions and, given also its extensive utilization within feminist (and other social) theory, it seems necessary to employ it.

2. The most sustained attempt to date to extract a theory of freedom from Foucault is perhaps Dumm's. Dumm makes a strong case that Foucault effectively challenges the "liberal" notion of the "democratic individual" as "the exclusive site of freedom" (1996, 5). However, his work does not explore issues of freedom raised by an alternative conception of the self, such as Beauvoir's, that does not neatly correspond with the liberal model.

3. The embarrassing evidence of Foucault's own youthful embrace of phenomenology has to be deliberately expunged from the author's presentation of his "work." Thus, in an interview published as late as 1983 (the year prior to his death), Foucault referred to *Madness and Civilization* as his "first" book ([1983] 1988, 23). In doing so this man, who claimed he wrote "to have no face" ([1969] 1972, 17), deliberately (mis)presented his "work" so as to exclude from it his earliest, and still phenomenologically influenced, book, *Mental Illness and Psychology* ([1954] 1976).

4. Thus James Miller observes, in the preface to his account of Foucault's life and work, that (perhaps contra Foucault himself) "I was forced to ascribe to Foucault a persistent and purposeful self, inhabiting one and the same body throughout his mortal life, more or less consistently accounting for his actions and attitudes to others as well as himself, and understanding his life as a teleologically structured quest" (1993, 7).

5. The English translator of *The Second Sex,* H. M. Parshley, has unfortunately translated Beauvoir's chapter heading "*Formation*" as "The Formative Years," thus weakening the notion of an active production of the self implied by the French term.

6. These relationships may sometimes give rise to the quite explicit *interests* that certain women have in complying with the norms of femininity. For example, for a dependent or low-earning housewife, the economic costs of a broken marriage that might result from resistant behavior can be catastrophic. Likewise, the refusal to submit docilely to forms of sexual harassment by a male superior at work can jeopardize many a woman's career. In some instances, contra Foucault, we may reasonably posit a woman as an interest-maximizing agent, in order to account for her complicity in her own continued personal subordination.

7. It is, I think, this omission that Nancy Hartsock has in mind when she observes (following Edward Said) that Foucault is "with power" rather than against it (1996, 36).

8. The French, *le regard,* has conventionally been rendered as "the look" in Sartre translations and scholarship, and as "the gaze" in the case of Foucault. While the two terms carry different resonances in English, these are the function of translation processes and would not be present for French readers.

9. Frantz Fanon also powerfully developed Sartre's account of shame, to explore the lived experiences of black embodiment in a predominantly white society ([1952] 1967). I discuss Fanon's relationship to Sartre more fully elsewhere (Kruks 1996).

10. Although girls from most social strata in the United States today are less constrained than were the middle-class women of Beauvoir's France, Beauvoir's observations generally still appear to hold. Iris Young has discussed a range of studies that show that girls (and women) still fail to extend their bodies, or to occupy space as fully as boys do; they throw, sit, walk, and carry things in typically timid and constricted "feminine" modalities. Young suggests that these are not merely different from masculine modalities, but are indicative of women's oppression: "Women in sexist society are physically handicapped. Insofar as we learn to live out our existence in accordance with the definition that patriarchal culture assigns to us, we are physically inhibited, confined, positioned, and objectified" (1990, 153).

11. An astounding number of products are aggressively marketed today that promise women "protection" against the dread embarrassments of leaks and odors. Deodorant tampons, special cleansers, and other such products abound on supermarket shelves and are heavily advertised.

12. The *content* of normalized femininity has, of course, shifted dramatically since Beauvoir's time, especially in the United States. But normalizing demands are no less intense today. Indeed, if the corset once constricted the body from without, today the demands not merely for slenderness but for a "well-toned" body necessitate an ever

greater interiorization of discipline (Bordo 1993). Sandra Bartky has suggested, with some plausibility, that women "have their own experience of the modernization of power, one which begins later but follows in many respects the course outlined by Foucault" (1990, 97). As women have achieved more freedom of movement, and as juridical male power over them has diminished, they have become subject to ever more demanding normalizing practices.

13. Beauvoir suggests this is also the case for lesbians, who, while refusing to engage in "normal" heterosexual behavior, still find themselves trapped in normalizing femininity ([1949] 1989, 404–24).

14. It is also to live in what Beauvoir (following Sartre) calls the mode of the "serious." As she wrote in *The Ethics of Ambiguity*, "The characteristic of the spirit of seriousness is to consider values as ready-made things" ([1947] 1967, 35) and so to refuse to accept responsibility for the values implicit in one's own actions. "The serious man's [*sic*] dishonesty issues from his being obliged ceaselessly to renew his denial of freedom. . . . The serious man must mask the movement by which he gives [values] to himself, like the mythomaniac who while reading a love-letter pretends to forget that she has sent it to herself" ([1947] 1967, 47).

15. Although his failure to make his own values explicit invites such a reading, I don't think Foucault himself draws this conclusion from his analyses. However, it is the demobilizing consequence drawn from his work by many feminists and other radicals, who fear to speak on certain topics lest they become implicated in power. Silence, it should be remembered, can equally implicate one in power.

REFERENCES

Bartky, Sandra. 1990. *Femininity and Domination*. New York: Routledge.
Beauvoir, Simone de. [1947] 1967. *The Ethics of Ambiguity*. Trans. Bernard Frechtman. New York: Citadel. Originally published as *Pour une morale de l'ambiguïté*. Paris: Gallimard.
———. [1949] 1989. *The Second Sex*. Trans. H. M. Parshley. Preface by Deirdre Bair. New York: Vintage. Originally published as *Le deuxième sexe*. Paris: Gallimard. Original English edition, New York: Knopf, 1952.
Bordo, Susan. 1993. *Unbearable Weight: Feminism, Western Culture, and the Body*. Berkeley: University of California Press.
Butler, Judith. 1997. *The Psychic Life of Power: Theories in Subjection*. Stanford, Calif.: Stanford University Press.
Dumm, Thomas. 1996. *Michel Foucault and the Politics of Freedom*. Thousand Oaks, Calif.: Sage.
Fanon, Frantz. [1952] 1967. *Black Skin, White Masks*. Trans. Charles Lam Markham. New York: Grove Weidenfeld.
Foucault, Michel. [1954] 1976. *Mental Illness and Psychology*. Trans. Alan Sheridan. New York: Harper Colophon.
———. [1969] 1972. *The Archaeology of Knowledge*. Trans. A. M. Sheridan Smith. London: Tavistock.

———. [1975] 1977a. *Discipline and Punish: The Birth of the Prison.* Trans. Alan Sheridan. London: Penguin Books.

———. 1977b. *Language, Counter-Memory, Practice: Selected Essays and Interviews.* Ed. Donald F. Bouchard. Ithaca, N.Y.: Cornell University Press.

———. [1979] 1984. "What Is an Author?" In *The Foucault Reader.* Ed. Paul Rabinow. New York: Pantheon. 101–20.

———. 1980. *Power/Knowledge: Selected Interviews & Other Writings, 1972–1977.* Ed. Colin Gordon. New York: Pantheon.

———. [1983] 1988. "Critical Theory/Intellectual History." In *Michel Foucault. Politics Philosophy Culture. Interviews and Other Writings 1977–84,* 17–64. Ed. Lawrence D. Kritzman. New York: Routledge.

Grosz, Elizabeth. 1994. *Volatile Bodies: Toward a Corporeal Feminism.* Bloomington: Indiana University Press.

Hartsock, Nancy. 1996. "Community/Sexuality/Gender: Rethinking Power." In *Re-visioning the Political.* Ed. Nancy Hirschmann and Christine DiStefano. Boulder, Colo.: Westview Press. 27–49.

Kruks, Sonia. 1990. *Situation and Human Existence: Freedom, Subjectivity and Society.* New York: Routledge.

———. 1996. "Fanon, Sartre, and Identity Politics." In *Fanon: A Critical Reader.* Ed. Lewis R. Gordon et al. Oxford: Blackwell. 122–33.

Miller, James. 1993. *The Passion of Michel Foucault.* New York: Simon and Schuster.

Sartre, Jean-Paul. [1943] 1956. *Being and Nothingness.* Trans. Hazel E. Barnes. New York: New Philosophical Library. Originally published as *L'être et le néant.* Paris: Gallimard.

Young, Iris M. 1990. *Throwing Like a Girl and Other Essays in Feminist Philosophy and Social Theory.* Bloomington: Indiana University Press.

4 Beauvoir on Mothers, Daughters, and Political Coalitions

LORI JO MARSO

> The relationships of women to their mothers and to other women—
> thus towards themselves—are subject to total narcissistic "black-out":
> these relationships are completely devalued. Indeed, I have never come
> across a woman who does not suffer from the problem of not being able
> to resolve in harmony, in the present system, her relationship with her
> mother and with other women.
>
> —Luce Irigaray

DISCUSSING HER DECISION to forgo motherhood, Simone de Beauvoir noted that "mother-daughter relationships are generally catastrophic" (qtd., Schwarzer 1984, 91). In the epigraph for this chapter, Luce Irigaray (1990, 95) speaks precisely to this observation. Irigaray laments the devaluation of vertical relationships between women (mothers and daughters), arguing that women must reclaim their female genealogies in order to act ethically and politically in establishing horizontal relationships of "sisterhood."[1]

I want to begin with and extend this insight by discussing ways feminists have received Beauvoir as a mother of feminism. I do not intend to undertake an exhaustive inventory of Beauvoir's reception among feminists. Instead, I read specific instances in Beauvoir's autobiography and autobiographical novels alongside her writings about motherhood and *A Very Easy Death* (Beauvoir 1965), the moving account of her own mother's deterioration and death, to explore Beauvoir's descriptions of the contradictions and ambivalence women experience in performing their femininity. I focus particularly upon difficulties women, including Beauvoir herself, encounter in breaking free from conventional confines of femininity to claim "authentic" freedom. I am especially interested in asking how daughters (and here I extend this to feminist daughters of Beauvoir) experience their mother's struggles within social and political conditions of patriarchy. I argue that what Irigaray calls "black-out" hinders feminist consciousness. Routine devaluation of female genealogy blinds us to the historical roots and complexities that influence our relationships to our mothers, to other women, to ourselves, and even to "canonical" women thinkers, such as Beauvoir.

Beauvoir as "Feminist Mother"

Marking a female genealogy as "intergenerational" does not limit the investigation to relationships between actual mothers and daughters, or even to relationships between living women (Cornell 2002, xviii). Varieties of mother/daughter tensions arise in an especially acute way in regard to Beauvoir as a "feminist mother." Yolanda Patterson reminds us that Beauvoir "laughingly" dismissed the idea that many feminists looked to her as a mother figure, noting "people don't tend to listen to what their mothers are telling them" (1986, 90). Patterson also acknowledges, however, that after Beauvoir's death several articles proclaimed her "the mother of the women's movement, the mother of all liberated women, whether or not they knew her name or her work" (ibid.).

When feminists claim Beauvoir as a feminist mother, we are confronted with a complex legacy detailed not only in philosophical work, but also in novels and autobiography. Through her letters, autobiography, and autobiographical fiction, Beauvoir deliberately opened up her life for others to scrutinize. In this work, contemporary feminists can witness how Beauvoir experienced and interpreted the complexities of her roles as woman, philosopher, and feminist.[2] The self-exploration that Beauvoir exhibited throughout her life is especially interesting when considered in the midst of what the *Women's Review of Books* has called the "Memoir Boom."[3] Nancy K. Miller notes the prolificacy of memoir as a genre for women writers and academic critics as a "renewed urgency to add the story of our lives to the public record" (Miller 1997, 982). Looking to Beauvoir's record of her life as a twentieth-century feminist philosopher has served as both inspiration and warning to feminists, especially in the years since her death.

Contemporary feminism's relationship to the legacy of Beauvoir's philosophy, life, and choices reflects deep divisions in regard to the reigning feminist debates on the significance of women's bodies, "feminine" sensibility, and the project of deciding whether "women" are the subject of feminism.

Beauvoir's questions and choices remain at the heart of these controversial and pressing issues. Under what conditions can women give voice to their desires, individually as well as collectively? Can we even speak of women?[4] Is it possible to identify and act on a feminine desire independent of the male construction of femininity?[5] Probing themes of conventional femininity as experienced by both Beauvoir and the women she creates in her fiction marks a return to our symbolic mother to reexamine continuing questions of freedom and choice in feminist politics.

Beauvoir's own experience of being a woman can be studied in her autobiographical fiction as well as in correspondence to friends and lovers. In fiction, she creates a number of women who are vulnerable, dependent, and conventionally feminine as well as women who strive to be independent but are continually in a state of turmoil brought on by the quest for this goal. The intense difficulty a woman experiences in becoming a desiring subject, for example, is vividly illustrated in Beauvoir's novel *She Came to Stay* (1982). Here we meet Françoise, the central character, struggling to define herself and negotiate her desires in relationship to three central persons in her life: Pierre, Xavière, and Gerbert. The situation in the novel, that of a sexual triangle, has been documented by Beauvoir herself and by her biographer, Deirdre Bair, as based on the real-life sexual triangle between Beauvoir (Françoise), Sartre (Pierre), and Olga Kosakiewitch (Xavière). Kosakiewitch, a fifteen-year-old student of Beauvoir's in 1933 (when Beauvoir was twenty-five), eventually married Jacques-Laurent Bost (portrayed in the novel as Gerbert), an important student of Sartre's and good friend to both Sartre and Beauvoir. The seduction of Gerbert by Françoise (enacting in literature the seduction of Bost by Beauvoir) is an excellent example of a woman's difficulty in giving voice to her own desire, even once she has recognized it.

Françoise, an independent and exceptional woman in every way, is quite able to recognize her desire, but given the constraints of how men and women are to behave in a patriarchal society, can she act on it? Her once "vague yearning" for Gerbert turns into a "choking desire" (Beauvoir 1982, 362). Françoise soon realizes that it would have to be she who would make the first move. "Owing to his youth and the respect he had always shown Pierre and herself, she could hardly expect him to take the initiative" (366). "She had always disregarded her dreams and her desires, but this self-effacing wisdom now revolted her. . . . Why did she not make up her mind to will what she hoped for?" (364). Françoise begins a conversation about the virtues of love and friendship. Gerbert claims that with a woman he can't be himself: "you can't go walking, you can't get drunk, or anything. . . . I prefer it when I can be just what I am with people" (366). Françoise assures Gerbert that he can be just who he is with her. "Oh you! You're like a man!" (363). Gerbert replies. Of course Françoise is an exceptional woman, but that hardly makes her just like a man.[6]

Exploring her options on how to approach Gerbert, Françoise thinks about a friend's experience with men. She, "a woman who takes" (Beauvoir 1982, 368), had affairs with many men, but no satisfaction. Françoise "loathed the thought" (ibid.) of acting in such an aggressive manner; likewise "she could not bear that he should give in to her out of kindness" (ibid.). The stakes in the dilemma are high. Beauvoir writes in *The Second Sex,* "It continues to be more difficult for a woman than for a man to establish the relations with the other sex that she desires. Her erotic and affectional life encounters numerous difficulties. In this matter the unemancipated woman is in no way privileged: sexually and affectionally most wives and courtesans are deeply frustrated. If the difficulties are more evident in the case of the independent woman, it is because she has chosen battle rather than resignation" (1989, 686).

Even more difficulties arise when the woman desires another woman in a male-dominated society. How is it possible that a woman could be a desiring subject when "the common opinion" is that "it is the man who conquers, who *has* the woman. . . . it is not admitted that she, like a man, can have desires of her own: she is the prey of desire" (Beauvoir 1989, 690). Though neither Beauvoir's autobiography nor *She Came to Stay* acknowledges her sexual relationship with Olga Kosakiewitch, Beauvoir's 1939 journal records relationships with three women, all émigrées from Eastern Europe—Kosakiewitch, Louise Védrine, and Natalie Sorokine (Simons 1992). Despite the fact that Beauvoir wasn't open about these aspects of her own sexuality, she takes a very progressive attitude in *The Second Sex.* Of lesbianism, she writes: "It is an attitude chosen in a certain situation—that is, at once motivated and freely adopted. No one of the factors that mark the subject in connection with this choice—physiological conditions, psychological history, social circumstances—is the determining element, though they all contribute to its explanation. It is one way, among others, in which woman solves the problems posed by her condition in general, by her erotic situation in particular" (424).

Lesbianism is considered an authentic choice, as "one attempt among others to reconcile her [woman's] autonomy with the passivity of her flesh" (Beauvoir 1989, 407). "The great mistake of the psychoanalysts is, through moralistic conformity, to regard it as never other than an inauthentic attitude" (406). Scholars studying Beauvoir's relationship with women find that they disrupt the boundaries of Beauvoir's heterosexual gender identity (see Simons 1992). Though *She Came to Stay* has often been read in terms of the difficulty the heterosexual couple encounters with the addition of a third party (see Barnes 1998), when we look beyond the heterosexual matrix, the novel's perspective changes. We have already noted that Françoise has tremendous difficulty voicing her desire for Gerbert. She has even more trouble recognizing and acting on her desire for Xavière. Out on the town together, arm in arm, "for [Xavière] did not dislike having people take them for a couple when they entered a place" (Beauvoir 1982, 246), Françoise wonders about her feelings for this younger woman: "Dancing had made her head spin a little. She felt Xavière's beautiful warm breasts against her, she inhaled her sweet breath. Was this desire? But what did she desire? Her lips against hers? Her body surrendered in her arms? She could think of nothing. It was only a confused need to keep forever this lover's face turned towards hers, and to be able to say with passion: 'She is mine'" (ibid.).

Even more pained than in her encounter with Gerbert, Françoise is at a complete loss with Xavière. She desires Xavière, yet she is unable to imagine the possibility of reciprocity. "How could she love me?" thought Françoise with pain. Frozen, unable to act, she worries over the consequences of her inability to be a fully desiring subject. "Had she [Xavière] hoped that Françoise would compel and force her love on her?" (Beauvoir 1982, 248). "What exactly did she want? Françoise had to guess; she had to guess everything: what Pierre felt, what was good, what was evil, and what she herself really and truly wanted. Françoise emptied her glass. She saw nothing clearly anymore, nothing at all. Shapeless wreckage lay all about her; within her a great emptiness and darkness throughout" (249).

The evening ends with Françoise feeling dismayed, confused, and disappointed. In writing of feminine sexuality, Beauvoir describes the erotic situation of the woman to be characterized by a fundamental ambiguity. She holds that woman's eroticism is much more "complex" than the male's reflecting "the complexity of the feminine situation" (Beauvoir 1989, 372). As Eva Gothlin has clarified, Beauvoir speaks of feminine desire as an "appeal" or a "calling out" to the other, a desire to be both "subject and object," to be within a relationship of mutual reciprocity and intersubjectivity (see Gothlin 1999; Lundgren-Gothlin 1996). This definition of feminine desire, one that marks a connection between an ethical position and the situation of women, is for Beauvoir a positive description. It is one that characterizes the ambiguity of the human condition and our relationship to freedom in that we are at one and the same time separate as well as interdependent beings. As many feminist theorists have noted, Beauvoir understands freedom to be experienced with others, rather than alone, and as both socially situated and conditioned (as opposed to absolute) (see Kruks 1995). The fundamental reality of women's situation is such that she finds herself within structures of oppression; her existence is shaped "not only by her own project but by the practices, institutions, and values of the world into which she is born" (90).

Given the example of a descriptive and compelling novel that shows the difficulty for an *emancipated* woman to recognize and act on her desire, we might wonder at the difficulty of achieving feminist consciousness in our most intimate relationships. Indeed, posthumous revelations about our feminist mother reveal that she cannot play the part of the independent woman all the time, *nor does she necessarily want to.* After Beauvoir's death in 1986, feminists began to react to significant new information regarding the gaps between Beauvoir's presentation of herself and the self she revealed in private letters and diaries. Though Beauvoir was certainly a model of the independent woman—as a scholar, a feminist, a political activist, and a woman who created new relationships outside of marriage—her struggle to maintain this identity and this lifestyle was opened for scrutiny with the publication of private diaries and letters. Her "essential" relationship with Sartre was the object of study and comment as were other "contingent" affairs with both men and women (see Hawthorne 2000).

One of these "contingent" affairs lasted for five years. In 1947, during her travels to the United States while she was writing *The Second Sex*, Beauvoir met the American writer Nelson Algren, with whom she experienced a passionate love. When Beauvoir's private letters to Algren were published in 1998, feminists were offered a new (and for some, shocking) perspective on Beauvoir's private life as a woman and the complex development of her feminism (Beauvoir 1998). Many readers found it troubling that Beauvoir, our icon (a role Beauvoir herself rejected), seemed sometimes unable to act on her own desires. Some of the passages from these letters indicate that she might have subordinated herself to her demanding lover:

> I have to admit this dependence, and I do so willingly since I love you. . . . I should throw everything else away to spend a longer time with you. I could have a room of my own so you could work quietly and be alone when you would wish. And I should be so nice: I'll wash the dishes and mop the floor, and go to buy eggs and rum-cake by myself; I shall not touch your hair or cheek or shoulder without being allowed to do so; I shall try not to be sad when you'll be ill-tempered because of the morning mail or for any other reason; I shall not interfere with your freedom. (71)

Hanging out by the lake in Michigan or in Algren's grungy Chicago apartment "washing the dishes," "mopping the floor," refraining from touching her "husband's" "hair or cheek or shoulder without being allowed to do so," represents a most dramatic contrast with Beauvoir's busy Parisian life as writer, philosopher, editor, and longtime companion of one of the most famous philosophers of the twentieth century. Could Beauvoir be engaging in her own fantasies of ease, of immanence, of choosing the easy slopes? Or is she simply being ironic, knowing all the while that she would never think of engaging in such a domestic routine? Maybe the willful performance of the fantasy of immanence helps to remind us of the importance of choosing lives of action and of transcendence. Or, can assuming immanence, rather than having it imposed in perpetuity, embrace the ambiguity of sexuality, and of intimacy?

In light of the flurry of responses to these letters that worried over Beauvoir's choice to conduct her affair with a "macho know-nothing at the very time she was writing *The Second Sex*" (Robinson 1999, 4), we might recall that Beauvoir's own claims about a woman's sexuality and freedom were complex. Even in her letter above, she demands a "room of her own" so that Algren can work quietly. It is important to think through Beauvoir's descriptions of the ambiguity of the feminine condition within the context of the way Beauvoir describes the dilemmas framing an "emancipated" woman's life. She herself had to negotiate the competing demands of love and independence. In the section on "The Independent Woman," in *The Second Sex,* Beauvoir writes that man is not divided. The emancipated woman, however, "refuses to confine herself to her role as female, because she will not accept mutilation; but it would also be a mutilation to repudiate her sex" (1989, 682). "To renounce her femininity is to renounce a part of her humanity" (ibid.), but what can a woman do when to realize her femininity a woman must make herself "object and prey" (ibid.)?

Beauvoir convincingly argues that sexuality "is profoundly different—biologically, socially, and psychologically—for man and woman" (1989, 371).[7] The woman embodies the ambiguity of the human situation more clearly than does the man, for the woman has difficulty in assuming the role of subject and of object.

> The erotic experience is one that most poignantly discloses to human beings the ambiguity of their condition; in it they are aware of themselves as flesh and as spirit, as the other and as subject. This conflict has a more dramatic shape for woman because at first she feels herself to be object and does not

at once realize a sure independence in sex enjoyment; she must regain her dignity as transcendent and free subject while assuming her carnal condition—an enterprise fraught with difficulty and danger, and one that often fails. (402)

Sexual relations constitute an especially interesting test for women's subjectivity in that woman, while used to being a sexual object, must become a desiring subject in order to enjoy the carnal act. In this sense, woman is especially "divided against herself" (Beauvoir 1989, 377). Indeed, how can women become sexual subjects when it is considered obscene to speak of woman's desire?[8] At the same time, the ambiguity of the erotic situation reveals that women must sometimes willingly make themselves objects in order to enjoy the sex act. As Beauvoir clarifies, "to *make* oneself an object, to *make* oneself passive, is a very different thing from *being* a passive object" (379). Feminine desire, as Eva Gothlin has characterized it, is for Beauvoir a situation in which "you are both subject and object, with the limits separating you and me as both there and erased" (1999, 89).

Yet, the question remains: are women offered, and can they seize, the opportunities to express desire and affirm their subjectivity under patriarchy? Is it even possible to speak of women as desiring subjects (or as desiring to *make* themselves passive rather than *be* objects) when women have been *spoken of* only as objects of male desire? And most important, could exploring these contradictions of feminine desire, those of our mothers and our feminist mothers, help us to articulate a feminist consciousness? I will argue that feminist consciousness might arise from comprehending and situating women's concrete similarities in regard to the difficulties of giving voice to our desires. This begins with a reclaiming of feminist genealogy.

Simone and Françoise

Luce Irigaray has asked, and answered, a fundamental question about Beauvoir: "So what did Simone de Beauvoir do? She gave an account of her own life while backing it up scientifically. She never stopped recounting it, bravely, at every stage. In so doing she helped many women—and men?—to be more free sexually, especially by offering them a sociocultural role model, acceptable at that time, of a woman's life, a teacher's life, a writer's life, and the life of a couple. I think she also helped them to situate themselves more objectively in relation to different moments in life" (1993c, 9).

Most of all, Beauvoir demonstrated that for the independent woman in patriarchal society, movement toward a life of transcendence and freedom is experienced in tension with the temptation simply to accept and perpetuate the conventional life that society has chosen as appropriate for women.[9] Daughters experience these contradictions in looking to the lives of their mothers, just as feminists, in reading the life of Beauvoir, experience contradictory emotions. Uma Narayan articulates that mothers and mother-cultures (and feminist mothers) inspire "complicated emotional responses from their feminist daughters—love and fear, the desire to repudiate and the desire to understand and be understood, a sense of deep connection and a desperate desire for distance" (1997, 10). Contradictory pulls between feminist consciousness and feminine destiny are manifested in our response. Beauvoir notes the dilemma for the "independent woman" as that between "human" freedom and her "feminine" destiny (1989, 679–715). How can we articulate a feminist response?

Beauvoir turns to her mother's story (and here we meet Beauvoir's mother, Françoise) to probe more deeply into her own. Narayan has written of the difficulty of weaving a mother's story into one's own, telling it faithfully while also creating the space to claim one's own history and subjectivity.[10] "Telling the story of a person whose life is intertwined with one's own, in terms different from her own, is often a morally delicate project, requiring accommodation and tact and an ability to leave room for her account even as one claims room for one's own" (Narayan 1997, 9). How can one write the story of the mother, subject as we are to intergenerational rage and resentment? Drucilla Cornell argues that feminist attempts at "multicultural, intracultural, and transnational dialogues between women" would be greatly enhanced in facing up to this "intergenerational haunting between women" (2002, xix, 24). The haunting, manifested in a "grim wasteland of broken spirits, victims of their own internalized oppression" (xx), must be explored as a common thread in women's lives. This exploration could turn broken dreams into dignity and hope for our daughters that they may be propelled to realize greater freedom for themselves.

Within a searing critique of conventional ideals of motherhood, Beauvoir is able to reclaim her mother's dignity in recounting her story as work on female genealogy. She symbolizes her relationship with her mother in a way that allowed her mother the space to be both a mother *and* a woman; this marks Beauvoir's essay as engaged in the feminist work of reimagining our relationships with our mothers. I will argue that Beauvoir's work allows us to rethink motherhood in vital and feminist ways. It frees women from competing for the unique place occupied by the mother; it frees women to differentiate themselves from their mothers; and it frees women from forever being reduced to the maternal function.[11]

To situate Beauvoir in relationship to maternal genealogies may appear, at first glance, counterintuitive. Indeed, feminist scholars have documented and debated the ambivalence Beauvoir demonstrates in regard to femininity and the female body.[12] Criticism has focused on her negative description of female biological functions such as menstruation, lactation, pregnancy, and maternity. Many cite Beauvoir as male-identified, and as abhorring the female body. Others document that Beauvoir interrogates biological descriptions of sexuality, offering an alternative description of female biology as constituted within situation, an historical, sociological, political and economic context (Arp 1995; Ward 1995).

In the view I offer here of Beauvoir's description of maternity and the mother/daughter bond in particular, Beauvoir is understood to be discussing the body not as a thing, but as a situation (1989, 34). Beauvoir makes clear that the body is always lived in by the subject; the meaning that biological "facts" take on is "dependent on a whole context" (ibid.). As examples, Beauvoir undermines the "naturalness" or inevitability of heterosexuality and reproduction. She insists, even, that no maternal "instinct" exists. "The word hardly applies, in any case, to the human species. The mother's attitude depends on her total situation and her reaction to it [and] this is highly variable" (511).

Though Beauvoir made the choice to not become a mother, she writes of the maternal bond from her perspective as a daughter. When she finds that she must confront her mother's deterioration and death from cancer, her relationship to the female body is tested in the most personal of contexts. *A Very Easy Death* negotiates Beauvoir's fear of her mother, of her mother's body, of becoming too *like* her mother, of the compulsion toward motherhood and the social and political roles that govern its expression. Coming into close contact with her mother's body in the hospital horrifies her: "The sight of my mother's nakedness had jarred me. No body existed less for me: none existed more. As a child I had loved it dearly; as an adolescent it had filled me with an uneasy repulsion: all this was perfectly in the ordinary course of things and it seemed reasonable to me that her body should retain its dual nature, that it should be both repugnant and holy—a taboo. But for all that, I was astonished at the violence of my distress" (1965, 19–20).

Unsurprisingly, Françoise de Beauvoir made frequent appearances in her daughter's dreams: "She blended with Sartre, and we were happy together. And then the dream would turn into a nightmare: why was I living with her once more? How had I come to be in her power again? So our former relationship lived on in me in its double aspect—a subjection that I loved and hated. It revived with all its strength when Maman's accident, her illness and her death shattered the routine that then governed our contacts" (1965, 103).

Beauvoir's experience of her own femininity as well as her political choices can be said to be framed by her rejection of the life trajectory of her conventional mother. Beauvoir finds maternal love comforting and whole, but also oppressive, suffocating, a threat to her own (the daughter's) sense of self. Beauvoir fears that a life spent redefining the meaning of being a woman, philosophically and personally, could be jeopardized by the paralysis and fear she feels in her mother's presence.

Simultaneously, though, Beauvoir has been inspired by her mother's life; the very constraints contained within it have motivated her to desire something different. In autobiographical writings Beauvoir recounts that her mother was always a model, usually one she did not wish to emulate. Elaine Marks notes that one might "sense that [Beauvoir's] revolt against the despicable bourgeoisie is, in part, an outgrowth of her revolt against Françoise de Beauvoir" (1973, 101). Witnessing her work in the home, seeing her personality strangled, taught the "dutiful" daughter to desire another kind of life. "One afternoon I was helping Mama to wash up; she was washing the plates, and I was drying; through the window I could see the wall of the barracks, and other kitchens in which women were scrubbing out saucepans or peeling vegetables. Every day lunch and dinner; every day washing-up; all those hours, those endlessly recurring hours, all leading nowhere: could I live like that?" (Beauvoir 1986, 104).

The hardships of her mother's life, the constant denial of her desire, and the effects that denial had on herself and her sister made Beauvoir firm in the belief that she would reject that life trajectory. In her *Memoirs of a Dutiful Daughter,* it is clear that Beauvoir sees motherhood as a kind of trap with the potential to suck her back into the bourgeois existence she so fears and loathes:

> I had long ago decided to devote my life to intellectual labours. Zaza shocked me when she declared, in a provocative tone of voice: "Bringing nine children into the world as Mama has done is just as good as writing books." I couldn't see any common denominator between these two modes of existence. To have children, who in their turn would have more children, was simply to go on playing the same old tune *ad infinitum;* the scholar, the art-

ist, the writer, and the thinker created other worlds, all sweetness and light, in which everything had purpose. (1986, 140–41)

The very fact that her mother's life consisted of a daily denial of what Beauvoir calls "awkward truths" was enough to convince her that "bourgeois marriage is an unnatural institution" (1965, 36). Years of betrayal by her husband, compounded by having to "give up many of the things she had dreamt of" (34), took its toll on Françoise de Beauvoir's spontaneity. When the mother is taught to deny her own desire, the maternal can ultimately be nothing other than a space of confinement and repression. Beauvoir remembers that there was an expression her mother employed that the family found vexing. She would begin her sentences "I certainly have the right." Beauvoir surmises that this phrase revealed her mother's "want of self-assurance," that "her desires did not carry their own justification with them" (39). As Beauvoir puts it, her mother "*lived* against herself": "She had appetites in plenty: she spent all her strength in repressing them and she underwent this denial in anger. In her childhood her body, her heart and her mind had been squeezed into an armour of principles and prohibitions. She had been taught to pull the laces hard and tight herself. A full-blooded, spirited woman lived on inside her, but a stranger to herself, deformed and mutilated" (42–43).

Beauvoir wonders how things would have been different with her mother had she lived her life as a free and desiring subject. Beauvoir recalls her mother's spontaneous smile, one exhibited far too infrequently, that ironically returns at the moment of sure death: "Both of us, my sister and I, had the same thought: it was that same smile that had dazzled us when we were little children, the radiant smile of a young woman. Where had it been between then and now?" (1965, 50).

The young Simone linked that smile with her parents' love, thinking it was "associated in some mysterious way with that bedroom she had just left" (1965, 34). But steadily, Beauvoir's mother had eased herself into a "successful marriage, two daughters who loved her dearly, some degree of affluence," hardly regretting that her husband's "wishes always came before hers," becoming quite capable of "selfless devotion" (34–35). Despite being "cut off from the pleasures of the body, deprived of the satisfactions of vanity, tied down to wearisome tasks that bored and humiliated her" (37), Françoise de Beauvoir kept up a "forced optimism" (38). Eventually, the Beauvoir family's declining fortune forced Simone's mother to look after the house without a servant. Beauvoir reports that her mother loathed the housework: "It is a pity that out-of-date ideas should have prevented her from adopting the solution she came round to twenty years later—that of working away from the home" (35). Wishing her mother could have experienced this slight degree of freedom, Beauvoir laments that "she would have escaped a degree of dependence that tradition made her think natural but that did not in the least agree with her nature" (36).

This insight, that freedom is constituted by situation, is aptly demonstrated in the analysis Beauvoir makes of her own mother's life. Had the situation for women in World War I France been more open, had Simone's mother been forced to go to work, had she come around herself to the solution of working away from the home earlier, she might have been "better equipped to bear the frustration that she had to put up with" (1965, 36). In fact, Françoise might have been a totally different kind of mother had her situation been different.

Can Beauvoir Teach Us about Political Coalition?

Beauvoir neglects to speak of a political strategy that would spur women toward a movement of emancipation, concentrating instead on individual difficulties women experience in recognizing themselves as complete and whole subjects able to desire love, freedom, even sexual satisfaction. Indeed, Michèle Le Doeuff notes, "The American Women's Liberation Movement, the French MLF of the 1970s and their equivalents in the other developed countries have not necessarily regarded *The Second Sex* [or Beauvoir's other works] as their *What Is to Be Done?* . . . nor would [Beauvoir] have liked it if they had" (2000, 43). If this is the conclusion, then what does Beauvoir have to say to feminists today? What can feminists learn from Beauvoir?

In marking out our own desires to transcend woman's body as inessential object, and articulating woman's desire to constitute herself as a desiring subject, Beauvoir simultaneously shows us how to be a woman subject among other women. Offering us her life as a model and her work as a collection of philosophy, fiction, and autobiography, and breathing life into the experiences of countless other women, Beauvoir shows us how we can perceive ourselves as women in the company of the experiences of other women. Though gender "is not always constituted coherently or consistently in different historical contexts," and "gender intersects with racial, class, ethnic, sexual, and regional identities" (Butler 1990, 3), the study of Beauvoir's life and work presents the possibility of understanding the conditions that produce diversity as well as those that establish the possibility of a unity of women. Le Doeuff calls this a kind of "minimum consensus:"

One can know oneself as a woman by being among women and through concern about what happens to other or to all women. Thus we saw lesbians joining in the struggle for contraception and abortion on demand, women who had the means to "get by" anyway calling for their legalization and reimbursement by social security, women without children setting up organizations for building crèches, single women showing their concern for the daily problems of housewives and Western women being appalled by clitoridectomy or the forced wearing of the chador. This is what replaced nail varnish and the acknowledgement of the lord and master in women's consciousness of self: a sense of being women because they wanted more freedom, a better life and dignity for all women. (2000, 45–46)

When Beauvoir frames women's desires in terms of the reaching out toward freedom and the obstacles encountered in that reaching (as well as how situation affects the possibility of reaching out), she returns us to a paradigm of seeking freedom on women's own terms, rather than seeking equality on male terms. Reading *The Second Sex,* Beauvoir's novels, and her letters, we are invited into the company of scores of women (as well as Beauvoir herself) engaged in seeking freedom while butting up against conventions of femininity. Describing ourselves as women under these circumstances does not demand that we inscribe certain characteristics to feminine desire, nor does it indicate anything essential about being a woman. Instead, it calls us to see ourselves as part of a community of beings who are blocked on the path to freedom. Moreover, it asks us to come together as a community seeking freedom without offering up a blueprint of how that might be accomplished or under whose name one might gather.

We might think of Beauvoir's discomfort with her mother's choices (as well as our own uneasy relationship to Beauvoir's choices) in light of the way she articulates the difficulty of choosing freedom and the attraction of the easy slopes. For Beauvoir, her mother's body represents immanence, decay, and the impossibility of transcendence, as well as the domain of choices her mother made, or failed to make. The "violence" of Beauvoir's "distress," however, does not manifest itself in repulsion for her mother, the other within herself. Rather than seek to expel the other, especially at this dangerous moment of recognition, Beauvoir feels compassion. She writes,

I talked to Sartre about my mother's mouth as I had seen it that morning and about everything I had interpreted in it—greediness refused, an almost servile humility, hope, distress, loneliness—the loneliness of her death and her life—that did not want to admit its existence. And he told me that my own mouth was not obeying me any more: I had put Maman's mouth on my own face and in spite of myself, I copied its movements. Her whole person, her whole being, was concentrated there, and compassion wrung my heart. (1965, 31)

Here Beauvoir recognizes that she has her mother's mouth "in spite of" herself; it even copies the movements of its progenitor. She struggles with her relationship to her mother, thinking through her mother's limited choices as well as the constraints of the body, in much the same way feminists have had to deal with Beauvoir's legacy. Certain discomforts are aroused when we are suddenly faced with the fact that Beauvoir the feminist also struggled with understanding her mother's life and resisting conventional models of femininity. In Beauvoir's life, we witness the uncomfortable reality that ontological freedom never exists independently of social and political freedom.

In *The Second Sex,* Beauvoir emphasizes that freedom cannot be gained through personal choice but only through a process of complex social transformation. In her introduction, she speculates on why women do not say "We" in regard to ourselves and our common interests: "Women lack concrete means for organizing themselves into a unit that can stand face to face with the correlative unit. They have no past, no history, no religion of their own; and they have no such solidarity of work and interest as that of the proletariat. . . . They live dispersed among the males, attached through residence, housework, economic condition, and social standing to certain men—fathers or husbands—more firmly than they are to other women" (1989, xxv).

Women are dispersed among various classes and races; they have "no past, no history, no religion of their own." Racial and class attachments prevent women from organizing into a unified movement under a singular umbrella. Moreover, and possibly most important, women's *emotional* attachments seem to separate them from each other, often attaching them to certain men—their husbands, their brothers, their sons, their fathers. These subjective/psychological aspects of women's emotional bonds reinforce the objective aspects of women's oppression. Choosing freedom, it turns out, is an arduous task, next to impossible for the *individual* woman. As Sonia Kruks puts it: "If woman is to become a free existent (and indeed if male freedom is to be increased), the process of change will have to commence from the radical transformation of the institutional aspects of woman's situation. Marriage, motherhood, her exclusion from economic and public activity, all will have to be extensively transformed" (1987, 117).

I have suggested here that the transformation might begin with the recognition of common struggles women encounter. Irigaray calls this acknowledgment "sisterhood," but Audre Lorde cautioned against believing that an invocation of "sisterhood" will necessarily foster solidarity:

> At home, my mother said, "Remember to be sisters in the presence of strangers." She meant white people, like the woman who tried to make me get up and give her my seat on the Number 4 bus, and who smelled like cleaning fluid. At St. Catherine's, they said, "Be sisters in the presence of strangers," and they meant non-catholics. In high school, the girls said, "Be sisters in the presence of strangers," and they meant men. My friends said "Be sisters in the presence of strangers," and they meant the squares. But in high school, my real sisters were strangers; my teachers were racists; and my friends were that color I was never supposed to trust. (1982, 81)

Lorde's autobiography forces us to think about location and coalition. In charting the barriers and boundaries she experiences as a woman, a lesbian, an African American of West Indian descent, she makes it clear that sisterhood doesn't make sense as an abstract or universal concept. As a child, Lorde was taught to see difference as a threat (which it was within her racist environment), not realizing that one can make coalitions with others unlike oneself. As readers, we witness her struggle to find a new spelling of her name as Zami, the Carriacou name for women who work together as friends and lovers.

I have made the claim in this essay that it is essential to investigate maternal genealogies, literal and metaphorical, in order even to begin to effect the change in consciousness required for women to think of each other as political allies, as friends, and as lovers. Looking to our mothers' lives and the lives and legacies of our feminist mothers acknowledges our vertical bonds, clearing the path toward forging horizontal ones. Beauvoir's struggles within her life, for example with her mother, with sexual attraction, with love, and with conventional definitions of womanhood, might inspire us, publicly and in concert with others, to speculate on the links between feminist consciousness and political action. Looking to the lives of other women, our mothers as well as women whose lives are mostly radically unlike our own, is an instigating factor inspiring feminist consciousness *toward* political coalition and action. If women could see links between their lives and their mother's lives, themselves and other women, we might avoid the "black-out" referred to by Irigaray in the opening epigraph to this essay. If we understand women's commonality as emanating from struggles to speak our desires and win our freedom (rather than as essence or fixed identity), women, however differently situated as subjects, might act together in common cause to end their shared oppression.

Maybe we expected more from our feminist mother? We should remember Beauvoir's descriptions of the difficulty of offering freedom to one's daughters while continuing to live within male definitions of philosophy, language, and self. Recognizing that we are deeply ensconced in relationships of patriarchy, Irigaray urges us to revalue vertical relationships toward the feminist project of positing horizontal ones:

> If we are not to be accomplices in the murder of the mother we also need to assert that there is a genealogy of women. Each of us has a female family tree: we have a mother, a maternal grandmother and great-grandmothers, we have daughters. Because we have been exiled into the houses of our husbands, it is easy to forget the special quality of the female genealogy; we might even come to deny it. Let us try to situate ourselves within that female genealogy so that we can win and hold on to our identity (1993c, 9).

It may give us pause to realize that Beauvoir fantasized about being a mother only under conditions in which men were completely absent. "When we played games, I accepted the role of mother only if I were allowed to disregard its nursing aspects.... I accepted the discreet collaboration of my sister whom I high-handedly assisted in the bringing up of her own children. But I refused to allow a man to come between me and my maternal responsibilities: our husbands were always abroad" (1986, 56). Must husbands be "abroad" in order for women to recognize and value their relationships with other women, both vertically (with mothers) and horizontally (with each other)? According to the reading of Beauvoir presented here, feminist practice, if it is to be transformative, must posit the relation to the other woman as the privileged interlocutor.

NOTES

1. As Irigaray suggests, "This world of female ethics would continue to have two vertical and horizontal dimensions: Daughter-to-mother, mother-to-daughter; among women, or among 'sisters.' In some way, the vertical dimension is always being taken away from female becoming. The bond between mother and daughter, daughter and mother, has to be broken for the daughter to become a woman. Female genealogy has to be suppressed, on behalf of the son-Father relationship, and the idealization of the father and husband as patriarchs. But without a vertical dimension . . . a loving ethical order cannot take place among women" (1993b, 108).

2. Beauvoir makes the case that circumstances of an individual life *necessarily* illuminate the lives of others. She says she wants to describe the realization of her "vocation as a writer" arguing that the "individual case" reveals much more than "generalized abstractions" (1984, 8).

3. *The Women's Review of Books* (1996, 5) chronicles an "avalanche of published memoirs by women in recent years."

4. Debates within contemporary feminism raise questions concerning the political as well as the philosophical risks of speaking of "women" as a coherent identity. Elizabeth Spelman identifies the political paradox at the heart of feminism: "Any attempt to talk about all women in terms of something we have in common undermines the attempt to talk about the differences among us, and vice versa. Is it possible to give the things women have in common their full significance without thereby implying that the differences among us are less important? How can we describe those things that differentiate women without eclipsing what we share in common?" (1988, 3).

5. Beauvoir explains in *The Second Sex* that to desire is man's domain as *subject;* woman is merely the *object* of his attention. See especially chapter 14, "Sexual Initiation," in *The Second Sex*. Here Beauvoir offers numerous examples of how men and women differently experience the sexual act. The man is the "*subject* as opposed to *objects* that he perceives and *instruments* he manipulates; he projects himself toward the other without losing his independence; the feminine flesh is for him a prey" (1989, 371).

6. Of this scene Toril Moi writes that "her exceptional position as a woman who can deal with men on an equal footing, that is to say without making them feel ill at ease, is confirmed when Gerbert compares her to one of the boys. . . . Such a discursive position puts her in a double bind, preventing her at once from flirting like a female and from speaking (or grabbing hands) like a man" (1994, 137–38).

7. Two recent books focus on Beauvoir's ethics as related to her emphasis on love and sexual desire. See Bergoffen (1997) and Vintges (1996). A focus on Beauvoir's sexuality is also central to the collection edited by Melanie C. Hawthorne (2000).

8. Since the 1970s, feminists have thought about the implications of theorizing from the perspective of the varieties of feminine desire. What would the world look like if the Other (as Beauvoir has it), or the unsignifiable (in Irigaray's sense), would speak in the language of her own desire? See De Lauretis (1994) and Milan Woman's Bookstore Collective (1990). Feminists gathered in the Milan Women's Bookstore Collective assert that for philosophers and politicians within the tradition that extols the universality of civil, human, and individual rights "female difference is indecent" (115). As Beauvoir notes, "the term 'female' is derogatory not because it emphasizes women's animality, but because it imprisons her in her sex" (1989, 3). It comes as no surprise, then, that a woman encounters "real difficulty" "acknowledging the immensity of a [sexual] desire she has no way of putting forward, openly, in full sight of society, without the disguise of some female virtue" (Milan Woman's Bookstore Collective, 115).

9. Beauvoir writes in *The Second Sex:* "It is man's good fortune—in adulthood as in early childhood—to be obliged to take the most arduous roads, but the surest; it is woman's misfortune to be surrounded by almost irresistible temptations; everything incites her to follow the easy slopes; instead of being invited to fight her own way up, she is told that she has only to let herself slide and she will attain paradises of enchantment. When she perceives that she has been duped by a mere mirage, it is too late; her strength has been exhausted in a losing venture" (645).

10. In her analysis of her identity as a "Third World feminist," Uma Narayan

stresses the importance of understanding our relationships to our mothers and our mother-cultures in the struggle for feminist consciousness. She writes, "For many of us, women in different parts of the world, our relationship to our mothers resemble our relationships to the motherlands of the cultures in which we were raised. Both our mothers and our mother-cultures give us all sorts of contradictory messages, encouraging their daughters to be confident, impudent, and self-assertive even as they attempt to instill conformity, decorum, and silence, seemingly oblivious to these contradictions" (1997, 8). To achieve feminist consciousness, one must be willing to acknowledge this ambivalence and rewrite our own stories. "Feminist daughters often have accounts of their mother cultures that differ in significant ways from the culture's own dominant account of itself. . . . Re-telling the story of a mother-culture in feminist terms . . . is a *political* enterprise" (10).

11. See Margaret Whitford's chapter "Maternal Genealogy and the Symbolic" (1991, 75–97).

12. Kristana Arp and Julie K. Ward have claimed that Beauvoir's seemingly negative remarks about female biology have been misinterpreted. See their essays in *Feminist Interpretations of Simone de Beauvoir* (Arp 1995; Ward 1995) for a context describing the negative interpretations of Beauvoir's work on female biology as well as an alternative interpretation, one with which this essay agrees, emphasizing Merleau-Ponty's influence on Beauvoir's development of the concept of the female body as a situation.

REFERENCES

Arp, Kristana. 1995. "Beauvoir's Concept of Bodily Alienation." In Simons 1995, 161–77.

Barnes, Hazel. 1998. "Self-Encounter in She Came to Stay." In *Simone de Beauvoir: A Critical Reader.* Ed. Elizabeth Fallaize. London: Routledge. 157–82.

Beauvoir, Simone de. 1965. *A Very Easy Death.* New York: Pantheon.

———. 1982. *She Came to Stay.* London: Fontana Paperbacks.

———. 1984. *The Prime of Life.* New York: Penguin.

———. 1989. *The Second Sex.* Trans. H. M. Parshley. New York: Random House.

———. 1986. *Memoirs of a Dutiful Daughter.* New York: Penguin.

———. 1998. *A Transatlantic Love Affair: Letters to Nelson Algren.* New York: New Press.

Bergoffen, Debra B. 1997. *The Philosophy of Simone de Beauvoir: Gendered Phenomenologies, Erotic Generosities.* Albany: State University of New York Press.

Braidotti, Rosi. 1989. "The Politics of Ontological Difference." In *Between Feminism and Psychoanalysis.* Ed. Teresa Brennan. London: Routledge. 89–105.

Burke, Carolyn, Naomi Schor, and Margaret Whitford, eds. 1994. *Engaging with Irigaray.* New York: Columbia University Press.

Butler, Judith. 1990. *Gender Trouble: Feminism and the Subversion of Identity.* New York: Routledge.

Cornell, Drucilla. 2002. *Legacies of Dignity: Between Women And Generations.* New York: Palgrave.

De Lauretis, Teresa. 1994. *The Practice of Love: Lesbian Sexuality and Perverse Desire.* Bloomington: Indiana University Press.

Gothlin, Eva. 1999. "Simone de Beauvoir's Notions of Appeal, Desire, and Ambiguity and Their Relationship to Jean-Paul Sartre's Notions of Appeal and Desire." In "The Philosophy of Simone de Beauvoir," ed. Margaret A. Simons, special issue, *Hypatia* 14, no. 4 (Fall): 83–95.

Hawthorne, Melanie C., ed. 2000. *Contingent Loves: Simone de Beauvoir and Sexuality.* Charlottesville: University Press of Virginia.

Irigaray, Luce. 1985. *This Sex Which Is Not One.* Trans. Catherine Porter. Ithaca: Cornell University Press.

———. 1990. "Women's Exile." Interview with Luce Irigaray. Trans. Couze Venn. In *The Feminist Critique of Language: A Reader.* Ed. Deborah Cameron. New York: Routledge. 80–96.

———. 1993a. "Body against Body: In Relation to the Mother." In *Sexes and Genealogies.* Trans. Gillian C. Gill. New York: Columbia University Press. 7–21.

———. 1993b. *An Ethics of Sexual Difference.* Trans. Carolyn Burke and Gillian C. Gill. Ithaca: Cornell University Press.

———. 1993c. *Je, Tu, Nous: Towards a Culture of Difference.* Trans. Alison Martin. New York: Routledge.

Kruks, Sonia. 1987. "Simone de Beauvoir and the Limits to Freedom." *Social Text* 17:111–22.

———. 1995. "Simone de Beauvoir: Teaching Sartre About Freedom." In Simons 1995, 79–95.

Le Doeuff, Michèle. 2000. "Hipparchia's Choice." In *French Feminism Reader.* Ed. Kelly Oliver. New York: Rowman and Littlefield.

Lorde, Audre. 1982. *Zami: A New Spelling of My Name.* Freedom, Calif.: Crossing Press.

Lundgren-Gothlin, Eva. 1996. *Sex and Existence: Simone de Beauvoir's The Second Sex.* Hanover, N.H.: Wesleyan University Press.

Marks, Elaine. 1973. *Simone de Beauvoir: Encounters with Death.* New Brunswick, N.J.: Rutgers University Press.

Milan Woman's Bookstore Collective. 1990. *Sexual Difference: A Theory of Social-Symbolic Practice.* Bloomington: Indiana University Press.

Miller, Nancy K. 1997. "Public Statements, Private Lives: Academic Memoirs for the Nineties." *SIGNS* 22, no. 4:981–1015.

Moi, Toril. 1994. *Simone de Beauvoir: The Making of an Intellectual Woman.* Oxford: Blackwell.

Muraro, Luisa. 1994. "Female Genealogies." In *Engaging with Irigaray.* Ed. Burke, Schor, and Whitford. New York: Columbia University Press. 317–33.

Narayan, Uma. 1997. *Dislocating Cultures: Identities, Traditions, and Third-World Feminism.* New York: Routledge.

Patterson, Yolanda. 1986. "Simone de Beauvoir and the Demystification of Motherhood." *Yale French Studies* 72:87–105.

Robinson, Lillian. 1999. "Review of *A Transatlantic Love Affair.*" *Women's Review of Books* 16, no. 7 (April): 1, 3–4.

Schwarzer, Alice. 1984. *Conversations with Simone de Beauvoir.* New York: Pantheon.

Simons, Margaret A. 1992. "Lesbian Connections: Simone de Beauvoir and Feminism." *SIGNS* 18, no. 1 (Fall): 136–61.

Simons, Margaret A., ed. 1995. *Feminist Interpretations of Simone de Beauvoir.* University Park: Pennsylvania State University Press.

Spelman, Elizabeth. 1988. *Inessential Woman: Problems of Exclusion in Feminist Thought.* Boston: Beacon.

Vintges, Karen. 1996. *Philosophy as Passion: The Thinking of Simone de Beauvoir.* Bloomington: Indiana University Press.

Walker, Michelle Boulous. 1998. "Mother-Daughter Poetics." In *Philosophy and the Maternal Body.* New York: Routledge. 170–75.

Ward, Julie K. 1995. "Beauvoir's Two Senses of 'Body' in *The Second Sex.*" In Simons 1995, 223–42.

Whitford, Margaret. 1991. *Luce Irigaray: Philosophy in the Feminine.* New York: Routledge.

Women's Review of Books. 1996. "The Memoir Boom." Special Issue. July 13.

Zakin, Emily. 2000. "Bridging the Social and the Symbolic: Toward a Feminist Politics of Sexual Difference." *Hypatia* 15, no. 3 (Summer): 19–44.

5 Beauvoir and Ethical Responsibility

KAREN SHELBY

IN ONE OF SIMONE DE BEAUVOIR's autobiographical works (*Hard Times: Force of Circumstance, vol. 2, 1952–1962*), she claims, "I am not a woman of action." She follows with an avowal of her vocation: "my reason for living is writing." Beauvoir ends the paragraph with this statement: "I contented myself with giving what help I could when I was asked for it; certain of my friends did more" (Beauvoir [1965] 1992, 183). Her commentary is found in the context of a discussion of the Algerian war for independence from France, fought from 1954 to 1962 (Ruedy 1992, 156–94). Beauvoir felt very deeply about this conflict. She was outspoken in her opposition to the continuing efforts of France to retain this North African colony. She also took on the cause of Djamila Boupacha, a young Algerian woman tortured by French soldiers.

In publicizing the Boupacha case, and urging French citizens to act on their knowledge of the conduct of the Algerian war, Beauvoir was invoking a notion of collective responsibility for actions with which many were not directly connected. And yet, Beauvoir saw the burden of French citizenship as necessitating some kind of response to the Algerian war and especially the means adopted by the French military in fighting it. Her autobiographical statement and her address to French citizens lead to an examination of what she meant by action, and its link to collective responsibility, and what these concepts mean in the contexts of her writings and political involvement. Her understanding of these terms pushes us to look beyond the everyday actions we engage in, and to confront their ethical meanings in their political context. It also leads us to examine the demand of extraordinary times for understandings of the political responsibility we bear in those times. What happens when most people, in fact, fail to act? What collective responsibility is entailed by this failure? This was the problem that confronted, and disheartened, Beauvoir during the Algerian war. She was looking for some kind of widespread oppositional response, while most of her fellow citizens found a military resolution of the conflict acceptable.

Freedom of One, Freedom of All

Simone de Beauvoir published *The Ethics of Ambiguity* in the fall of 1947, two years after the end of World War II, and three years after the liberation of Paris. In this, one of her several specifically theoretical works, she establishes an ethical theory based in what she describes as the fundamental ambiguity of the human condition. What we all have in common as human beings, she says, is the perception of ourselves as subjects, of others as objects, and the difficulties that inhere in the recognition that for those "other" subjects, we are objects, and that they are themselves subjects in their own right. It is a given for Beauvoir that there is no higher power upon which humans can rely that will reveal or hide the meaning of human lives. Each person must make meaning out of the material of life. The disclosure of this meaning, or failure thereof, is found in the content of the actions each person undertakes.

While each subject exists for the disclosure of the meaning of her own life, she also exists in a world of other subjects, and one of the fundamental difficulties is that these "other subjects" are seen and treated merely as "others." It is this difficulty that must be confronted in the making of a meaningful life. Beauvoir says, "And it is true that each is bound to all, but that is precisely the ambiguity of his condition: in his surpassing toward others, each one exists absolutely as for himself; each is interested in the liberation of all, but as a separate existence engaged in his own projects" (1948, 112). In this statement is contained the individualism for which existentialism is known, although Beauvoir immediately establishes a link to the broader communities of others to which the individual belongs.

For Beauvoir, the overall goal out of which each person must make meaning of her life is the search for the conditions that will allow all people to choose freedom. She asserts, "An ethics of ambiguity will be one which will refuse to deny *a priori* that separate existants can, at the same time, be bound to each other, that their individual freedoms can forge laws valid for all" (1948, 18). However, this is difficult as the modern condition imposes constraints whereby "[m]en of today seem to feel more acutely than ever the paradox of their condition. They know themselves to be the supreme end to which all action should be subordinated, but the exigencies of action force them to treat one another as instruments or obstacles, as means" (8–9). Acting on this understanding of other humans as means to the accomplishment of one's own project, rather than humans with their own ends, establishes conditions of oppression (83).

Because oppression is a human creation, it is a particularly human responsibility to combat it, despite the naturalistic or essentialist guises that may obscure that responsibility (Beauvoir 1948, 81, 83). Of the "struggle against oppression," Beauvoir says that "every man is affected by this struggle in so essential a way that he can not fulfill himself morally without taking part in it" (88, 89). Here we see a fundamental ethical imperative. And although Beauvoir's statement of the problem may seem simplistic, her push toward the particulars of an individual's situation as the ground of the ethical content of lived existence complicates her theory and turns it in a political direction. Ethics gives the baseline imperative, that is, the extension of freedom to all, but it is politics that determines the possibilities for actions to be taken (89).

When Beauvoir asks which of the enemies of the "Arabian fellah," or peasant, must be confronted, or when she asks whether the interests of the French proletariat or colonized subjects of the French should take precedence, she is acknowledging her own complex confrontation with conflicts of class and colonialism, as well as that of her contemporaries (1948, 89). She is acknowledging that political claims are necessarily partial, unable to encompass the totality of a given situation. At the same time, her understanding that our choices are never finally determinate leaves room to make further claims that may or may not compete with claims previously made. In posing these questions that link ethics and politics, Beauvoir is also confronting that which she believes gives human freedom content and meaning, and that is the attempt, in the face of her understanding of intersubjectivity, to minimize the harm and maximize the opportunities for each individual's freedom, one's own and that of others. She does not believe that one's own freedom can be achieved by simply ignoring conditions that deny the freedom of others, and this is what she posits should motivate us to act ethically.

While one is free to choose the means, mode, and content of one's action, it is not ethical action unless it gestures in the direction of freedom for all. Failure to hold oneself to this standard would involve life lived on the mere order of being, given over to the superficiality of the here and now, and the realm of the necessary, the unthinking. On the other hand, engaging in ethical action would involve a move toward authentic existence, which is not only lived in the present but gestures toward the future, toward projects of freedom. At the same time, the choice, in existentialism, through one's actions to reject one's own freedom, or to reject that of others and also thereby curtail one's own freedom, is an open possibility, and it is against this that Beauvoir writes in her *Ethics*.

A Typological Heuristic, or Fifty Ways to Fail Your Freedom

Beauvoir presents several different types of persons and potential ways of living, some of which contravene her imperative that "[i]t is in the knowledge of the genuine conditions of our life that we must draw our strength to live and our reason for acting" (Beauvoir 1948, 9). In some way, each of these types represents a flight from recognition of the condition of ambiguity in which people live, or a failure to recognize the commitments to others that Beauvoir would have each of us acknowledge, until she discusses the potential that is manifest in the work of the artist and writer. According to Beauvoir, the artist and writer offer a means for humans to understand their ethical commitments through exercises of thought that may prepare them to act in the world. What is the same about all of these typologies is that they are descriptions of what persons may, through the choices they make, be or do at a particular moment in time, or perhaps over a longer period of time. However, people are not inherently of a certain type, and a person can, by virtue of the choices and actions she makes and undertakes, fall into one category or another, or overlap categories. In fact, looking at these "types" is most helpful as a heuristic that provides a means of concretizing her theory and showing examples of some of the potential pitfalls, and potential for its realization.

To begin with the hazards, the first type she calls the "sub-man," who is content with living only in the realm of being, unthinkingly and superficially in the present. The sub-man acts against the impulse to engage the world through ethical action, remaining in a cycle of stagnation and nothingness. What is particularly dangerous about the sub-man is that because that person chooses no project, he is open to the manipulation of others, for purposes that he does not choose (Beauvoir 1948, 43–44).

The "serious man" also rejects existence, but does so in such a way that "[h]e loses himself in the object in order to annihilate his subjectivity" (Beauvoir 1948, 45). This object is a project of sorts, and it can take many forms, but the crucial aspect of the life of the serious man is the subjugation of self in the service of an object that is unquestioned and taken as an unchanging given. For Beauvoir, the content of the project of freedom is constantly changing, and one chooses each day, each moment, what the content of that project will be. The serious man seeks precisely the comfort of an unchanging, unexamined basis for action and for this reason, the actions that follow are inauthentic.

This serious attitude can fall into that of "the nihilist," someone whose object becomes the pursuit of nothingness. This attitude is different from that of the sub-man in its cognizance that life must have an object beyond mere being. However, the failure of the object as pursued by the serious man leads to nihilism, and the object is then to "be nothing" (Beauvoir 1948, 52). Beauvoir asserts that the nihilist is both correct and tragically wrong: "The nihilist is right in thinking that the world *possesses* no justification and that he himself *is* nothing. But he forgets that it is up to him to justify the world and to make himself exist validly" (57).

Next, Beauvoir examines the type she calls "the adventurer." This person is constantly acting, but there is no purpose behind the action other than "action for its own sake" (Beauvoir 1948, 58). This person "finds joy in spreading through the world a freedom which remains indifferent to its content" (ibid.). Like the serious man, the adventurer acts, but the lack of a coherent project of freedom informing the action robs it of any ethical content.

The "passionate man" is like the serious man in his selection and adherence to an object, but whereas the serious man sees that object as separate, the passionate man believes that "it is disclosed by his subjectivity" (Beauvoir 1948, 64). Because he believes that this freedom is his alone, he does not hesitate to treat other humans as things, consigning them through thoughts and actions to the realm of fixed objects or tools in a personal search for an ostensibly higher aim (66).

The "critic" fails in the realm of epistemology. The failure is revealed in that "[h]e understands, dominates, and rejects, in the name of total truth, the necessarily partial truths which every human engagement discloses . . . and what he defines as objective truth is the object of his own choice" (Beauvoir 1948, 68–69). The critic, even when engaged solely in his own intellectual pursuits, makes the mistake of substituting his own truth for a universal truth that could only ever be partial, and which cannot be realized at the level of theory alone.

Against these types, Beauvoir upholds "the artist and the writer," who, when acting authentically, seek to reify existence, and to make meaning, but without attempting to assert thereby their own being as fixed. In this way, they avoid the trap of the sub-man; but the authenticity of the search for human existence, and the understanding of the partiality of the truths revealed through art, also lead them to avoid the pitfalls of the serious man, the passionate man, or the critic as they engage with the world (Beauvoir 1948, 69). One of the things Beauvoir believes the artist and writer can do through their works is encapsulate and potentially arrest the ongoing play of significations in a chosen situation, and freeze a moment of existence. Both the artist and writer as well as those who observe what they have created are potentially pulled out of the limited frame of their own subjectivity, opened to an experience of another subjectivity, and confronted with an alternate vision of existence. Through the push to see things from a different perspective, or perhaps the shock to one's subjectivity experienced through the writer's or artist's work, the person is confronted with a vision of life that is inclusive of more than merely the limited subjectivity of any one person. This opens up the possibility for a momentary means of bridging the difficult gap between subject and object that is the essence of the human condition, according to Beauvoir. This is beneficial in that it offers those who encounter the work(s) the opportunity to engage in an exercise of thought, preparing them to think and to act ethically when confronted with situations that demand it.

The last of Beauvoir's types is juxtaposed with the bad example of the "adventurer," whose action is without purpose, and is called by Beauvoir the "genuinely free man." The nebulous description is of someone "whose end is the liberation of himself and others" and who acts in such a way that the means to his desired end do not contravene that end (Beauvoir 1948, 60). The writer and artist are figures whose labors Beauvoir believes may help others to prepare themselves to become genuinely free women and men.

Action and Collective Responsibility

We must each decide which actions to take for ourselves, as "[e]thics does not furnish recipes any more than do science and art. One can merely propose methods" (Beauvoir 1948, 134). Beauvoir turns to politics as a necessary guide to ethical action, in the exploration and determination of what possibilities for action are presented, as well as in her understanding of action as open-ended in its result. Politics gives a structure to action but does not determine it. One is still responsible for the consequences of one's actions. Therefore, the ethical and the political work hand in hand for Beauvoir, since it is the ethical imperative of freedom for all that serves as the impetus to action.

Reading Beauvoir's novel *The Blood of Others,* published in France the year prior to her *Ethics,* contributes to an understanding of the development of her ethical theory. The trials of the characters she created, and their comprehension, incomprehension, achievements, and missteps, serve as a literary, and somewhat more concrete, precursor of the principles set out in *The Ethics of Ambiguity.* In this novel, Beauvoir presents some of the ruses her characters use in an attempt to fool themselves into believing they can avoid engaging the world, as well as the ways in which they positively engage or act in the world. These characters are confronted with choices that are more complex and therefore more lifelike, in comparison to the types mentioned above. The novel is set during World War II, and the background of action is a Resistance cell in France. The questions the protagonist must answer are whether or not—and how best—to act. The ultimate message is that one *must* act in order to live fully, even if those actions may have terrible repercussions. Abdication of responsibility by failing to act is the bad faith alternative that the protagonist of the novel must eventually reject.

To return to her *Ethics,* Beauvoir says of the motive force behind all ethical action, "It is desire which creates the desirable, and the project which sets up the end. It is human existence which makes values spring up in the world on the basis of which it will be able to judge the enterprise in which it will be engaged" (1948, 15). The judgment is determined both at the communal level, in the laws and precepts that societies establish as their guiding principles, and at an individual level, by the person contemplating the particular action in question. On the one hand, she says that we must all decide which actions to take for ourselves. We are free to act in ways that promote neither our own nor anyone else's project of freedom. On the other hand, in order to be a part of ethical action, that decision must take into account the presence of others, and the impact that the action(s) will have on those others. This moment of decision, and the form that it could take, is ostensibly left to the individual to shape, whether through positive action and the desire to claim one's own freedom, or through renunciation of the moment of acknowledgment and potential freedom, that is, in Beauvoir's terms, living in bad faith. It is also for her a question of politics, of the political context that enables choices. And as presented in *The Blood of Others,* it is most clearly seen in action that happens in concert with others.

What happens, however, when the "action" in concert is inaction? The political theorist who immediately and directly addressed this problem of modernity in its most horrific consequences is Hannah Arendt. In 1945, she wrote an essay originally entitled "German Guilt," republished under the title "Organized Guilt and Collective Responsibility." In this essay, Arendt examines the concepts of guilt and responsibility and their political import. At first, she looks at the deliberate conflation by the Nazis, engendered by the totalitarianism of the regime, of the guilty and the innocent. In such a regime, one is either committing crimes or complicit in their commission (Arendt [1945] 1994, 124). At the same time, Arendt wants to explore the idea of responsibility. Of some who were "sympathetic to Hitler," she says, "Who would dare to brand all these ladies and gentlemen of high society as war criminals? And as a matter of fact, they really do not deserve such a title. Unquestionably they have proved their inability to judge modern political organizations, some of them because they regarded all principles in politics as moralistic nonsense" (125). This understanding of responsibility entails a personal failure of political engagement, as opposed to a direct commission of a war crime. And yet, those individuals do bear a responsibility entailed by historical events.

Arendt finds that the failure of engagement in the public, political realm is that which is emblematic of "this modern type of man, who is the exact opposite of the 'citoyen' and whom for lack of a better name we have called the 'bourgeois'" ([1945] 1994, 130). Ultimately, Arendt turns to an "elemental shame," "of being human," and the "consequence that in one form or another men must assume responsibility for all crimes committed by men and that all nations share the onus of evil committed by others" (131). This translates politically to a necessary recognition and "genuine fear of the inescapable guilt of the human race," particularly by those who have undertaken the task of "fighting fearlessly, uncompromisingly, everywhere against the incalculable evil that men are capable of bringing about" (132). In this essay, and it is not surprising given its historical context, Arendt's rhetoric is rivetingly strong.

In a later essay, entitled "Collective Responsibility," Arendt draws a finer distinction between "moral and/or legal (personal) guilt," and "political (collective) responsibility" ([1968] 1987, 46). As in the previous essay, what she now calls collective responsibility is something to which humans are subject, through their condition of belonging to a community. Arendt describes the necessary conditions of "collective responsibility" as follows:

> I would say that two conditions have to be present for collective responsibility: I must be held responsible for something I have not done, and the rea-

son for my responsibility must be my membership in a group (a collective) which no voluntary act of mine can dissolve. . . . This kind of responsibility . . . is always political, whether it appears in the older form, when a whole community takes upon itself to be responsible for whatever one of its members has done, or whether a community is being held responsible for what has been done in its name. The latter case is of course of greater interest for us because it applies, for better and worse, to all political communities and not only to representative government. (45)

Arendt goes on to describe the responsibility for deeds committed by its predecessors that each government takes on. This is certainly true in the case of Algeria, in which past acts of colonization were at issue. However, for Simone de Beauvoir, the legacy also entailed present acts of torture that she perceived as being ignored by French citizens, while being committed by the French military in the name of all French men and women. This led her to attempt to confront those citizens with their responsibility for these acts, despite their distance from the commission of those acts.

Algerian War and Djamila Boupacha

While opposed to the violent maintenance of "Algérie française" from the beginning of the war, Beauvoir eventually took on a particular project that involved two goals. One was to remind the French people of the atrocities that were being committed in their name and to which many turned a blind eye, acts for which Beauvoir believed they were ultimately responsible as French citizens. The other was to bring about the release and vindication of Djamila Boupacha.

In February 1960, during the struggle for Algerian independence, Djamila Boupacha was imprisoned as a suspect in the planting of a bomb, later defused, in the café of the University of Algiers. She admitted involvement with the Algerian resistance forces, including having harbored agents in her house, but initially denied any involvement with the bomb at the café. Eventually, a confession was extracted from her under torture, which included submersion in water, electric shock, and rape with a bottle. The systematic torture of Algerians taken into custody was one of the central means of waging the "counter-terrorist" war of the French military forces (Sorum 1977, 113–29; Maran 1989). There was little accountability for these actions. They were allowed as a sort of necessary evil by the French colonizers and encouraged as a means of gathering intelligence by the military command. These actions were ignored by officials in France, who by this point wanted the conflict—which had spread across the Mediterranean into France—to be over, and France victorious. Boupacha's case would have been like many others, a quick trial followed by a guilty verdict based upon a confession that was the only evidence available, if not for her own courage, the intervention of Gisèle Halimi, a young French attorney known for her activism, and the involvement of Simone de Beauvoir.

In Boupacha's first interview with a magistrate, after more than a month of imprisonment, she had the temerity to make the request, "Notez que j'ai été torturée" [Note that I have been tortured] (Montreynaud 1995, 466), and to demand that she be examined by a doctor. Her accusations were greeted mainly with indifference by the magistrate, but Boupacha stood by her allegations of torture and declarations of innocence despite threats of both further torture to herself and harm to her family. At the same time, her brother wrote from Algeria to Halimi and asked her to take the case. Halimi agreed.

Part of the challenge for Halimi was the official resistance she knew she would encounter in both Algeria and France. This included restriction of her first trip to Algiers to forty-eight hours, a severe limitation given that Halimi would arrive on the seventeenth of May, Boupacha's hearing would take place on the eighteenth, and the dossier for her case would not be available for her lawyer to see on the day before the hearing. Halimi tried to have the visa extended, although it was not surprising to her that it was not, as "the frequency with which those lawyers who regularly pleaded in Algeria were interned, expelled, or arrested while going about the normal business of their calling pointed to a deliberate policy of ensuring that the farcical travesty which passed for justice there should continue unmolested" (Beauvoir 1962, 25). The harassment engendered by the attempt to maintain the colonial system was an impediment to Halimi's (and other attorneys') freedom as well, even though the lawyers could more or less continue in the exercise of the legal profession. Halimi worked through the courts initially to have the trial postponed to give adequate time to prepare a defense for the proceedings in Algeria, and eventually to have the trial moved to France, where an impartial judge might be found. The likelihood was also perhaps greater that the allegations of torture might be investigated by a French judge more removed from the immediacy of the conflict.

One of the first things that Halimi did upon returning to Paris from Algeria was to notify officials, all the way up to Charles de Gaulle, of the circumstances of Boupacha's case, including the allegations of torture. This she did in order to "destroy a myth and block a handy official loophole. Whenever such abuses are brought to the notice of those ultimately responsible for them, we hear the same old song: 'It's an Algerian affair; Paris knew nothing about it'" (Beauvoir 1962, 63). Halimi also contacted persons who had made known their opposition to France's conduct of the war, including Simone de Beauvoir. It was decided that they must arouse public sympathy, a not-insignificant task, as they must "overcome the most scandalous aspect of this whole scandalous affair—the fact that people *had got used to it.*" They concluded that "[t]he French had to be shocked out of their comfortable indifference to the Algerian problem" (65).

With this in mind, Beauvoir mobilized her social and intellectual capital and wrote a stirring letter intended to galvanize public opinion. The letter was published in the newspaper *Le Monde* on June 2, 1960, under the title, "In Defense of Djamila Boupacha." Beauvoir sought to confront the French people both with the horrific facts of Boupacha's torture and with their own complicity in the perpetuation of such practices in Algeria. Although Beauvoir was forced to substitute the word "belly" for the word "vagina" in the sentence that was to read, "They forced a bottle into her vagina," the severity of such a description of violation and torture was intended to provoke a reaction, and it made what was an incident like many others in Algeria a *cause célèbre* in France.

Beauvoir wrote of the ease with which the "heart-breaking cries of agony and grief that have so long been going up from Algerian soil—and indeed, in France as well—have failed to reach your ears, or if they have, have been so faint that it took only a little dishonesty on your part to ignore them" (1962, 10–11). Against this attitude, Beauvoir proposes in her *Ethics* that "only the freedom of others keeps each one of us from hardening into the absurdity of facticity" (1948, 71), offering a motive both self-interested and intersubjective for ethical action. In the context of the Algerian war and Djamila Boupacha's situation, the knowledge that practices such as torture were standard procedure for French troops should have outraged persons who considered themselves ethical human beings, but it did not.

It was left to Beauvoir, and writers, activists, and artists like her, to educate French women and men about, to use Arendt's term, the collective responsibility for those acts that membership in the community of French citizens had entailed to them. The fog of apathy that perhaps made their lives more comfortable also rendered them incapable of seeing their own humanity, in the sense outlined by Arendt, as well as the parallel humanity of the Algerians fighting for independence. The justice of the claims of the Algerians who had lived for more than a century under France's colonial rule, and who were fighting to throw it off, was an issue French citizens trusted to the same French officials who duplicitously affirmed that torture was not an accepted practice anymore in Algeria, then ignored evidence to the contrary, or condoned such conduct by the military. Beauvoir expected that her fellow citizens would examine for themselves what was happening in Algeria; she believed they would come to some decision as to the rightness or wrongness of what they found, and act.

As noted above, the particular action possible is dependent on the situation of the individual and upon politics, according to Beauvoir. She says that "here the question is political before being moral: we must end by abolishing all suppression; each one must carry on in his struggle in connection with that of the other and by integrating it into the general pattern. What order should be followed? What tactics should be adopted? It is a matter of opportunity and efficiency. For each one it also depends on his individual situation" (1948, 89). It is clear that in the context of Djamila Boupacha's case, Beauvoir expected that French women and men should act ethically by responding in some way in light of the burden of collective responsibility that their complicity had brought them.

In comparison to the revelations about the Holocaust and the genocidal intentions of the system of concentration camps that led Arendt to invoke an absolute judgment about the wrongness of those acts, and the culpability that humans in the conditions of modernity must bear for them, Beauvoir's absolute appeal is not as strong. In the face of government assurances that the Algerian war was necessary, particularly when it was explained as a civilizing mission (see Maran 1989), why should French citizens contest those claims? One reason that Beauvoir would give, of course, is that the goal of the war, that is, the maintenance of a colonized country as such, was unjust and impeded Algerians' ability to claim their freedom. Another would be that the conduct of the war, that is, the systematic use of torture, was wrong as well.

And yet for Beauvoir, there is a contradiction in her philosophical understanding that in a particular historical situation, the content of the action is not determined, alongside her insistence that in this case the opportunity to act was offered, and that she wanted French citizens to act with a certain antiwar agenda. Beauvoir believed that the freedom offered was not one of complacency (their own safe, comfortable, ersatz freedom as French citizens at home, sympathetic to those French citizens in Algeria) but something qualitatively different. To be free in this particular historical situation demanded the ethical commitment to end their complicity in the oppression of the Algerian people. The freedom offered through collective action was the antidote to French citizens' collective responsibility for the plight of the Algerian people under French colonization, and the conduct of the war being fought to maintain it.

Beauvoir recognized that "[o]ppression tries to defend itself by its utility . . . [but that] nothing is useful if it is not useful to man; nothing is useful to man if he is not in a position to define his own ends and values, if he is not free" (1948, 95). In this, Beauvoir was anticipating some of the objections to an independent Algeria, and some of its justifications as well. This suggests that political assessment is the constant companion of ethical action, and that citizens needed to let those politicians who continued to defend France's colony and its means of retention know that they would no longer accept this behavior or rationale. They could, and some did, do this through protests, petitions, and direct confrontation. They sought thereby to inspire "general revulsion" for the treatment of Djamila Boupacha and others similarly treated. But Beauvoir insists that this feeling is not enough, as "any such revulsion will lack concrete reality unless it takes the form of political action" (1962, 20).

Attempting to build on the revulsion her article had engendered, Beauvoir also organized a Djamila Boupacha committee to put pressure on French officials. Her goals as stated in *Le Monde* were: to obtain further postponement of Boupacha's trial, in order to have time enough to investigate Boupacha's allegations; to ensure that neither Boupacha's family nor witnesses favorable to her would be harassed, intimidated, or worse; and to see the torturers of the El Biar and Hussein Dey prisons, where Boupacha had been held, brought to justice (Beauvoir 1962, 65). While some public sympathy may have been aroused by the publicity given this case, official intransigence remained firmly in place. In her introduction to *Djamila Boupacha*, Beauvoir recounts the reaction of one official, the president of the Committee of Public Safety: "After all—as was delicately hinted by M. Patin . . .—Djamila Boupacha is still alive, so her ordeal cannot have been all that frightful. M. Patin was alluding to the use of the bottle on Djamila when he declared: 'I feared at first that she might have been violated *per anum*. . . . such treatment results in perforation of the intestines, and is fatal. But this was something quite different,' he added, smiling: clearly nothing of the sort could ever happen to *him*" (9).

It was this attitude of bland indifference that Beauvoir found impossible to accept. Patin was comfortable in the protection both from reflection and from responsibility that he believed his role in the bureaucracy provided. In the face of this, Beauvoir insisted that as both a French citizen and an official of the French government, he bore a responsibility that he refused to acknowledge. Relief that Djamila Boupacha was not dead rang false, when there were plenty of other allegations of torture that had resulted in death. Additionally, ignoring that Boupacha had suffered grievous harm was a way of evading the impetus to think and act.

Hannah Arendt described precisely this understanding of the world and one's place in it as characteristic of "the bourgeois," the antithesis to the active, engaged "citoyen" ([1945] 1994, 130). In an interview that she quotes, an employee at a concentration camp responds to a series of questions: "Q. Did you personally help kill people? A. Absolutely not. I was only paymaster in the camp. Q. What did you think of what was going on? A. It was bad at first but we got used to it. Q. Do you know the Russians will hang you? A. (Bursting into tears) Why should they? *What have I done?*" [Arendt's italics] (127). To this, Arendt replies, "Really he had done nothing" (ibid.). She goes on to delineate the responsibility he bore as a human for the atrocities of which all humans are capable, and the conditions that allowed him to believe he would be exempted from responsibility.

The themes are similar in the situation of the Algerian war. The French were "used to" the conflict and allegations of torture. And if confronted about their complicity in the conflict, most would probably have responded "What have I done?" But there is no free pass in life, according to Beauvoir. In asking regarding Djamila Boupacha, "Can we still be moved by the sufferings of one girl?" (Beauvoir 1962, 9), Beauvoir issued not just an imperative for empathy or thought, but a call to action. Her insistence that it is the fundamental tie between the self and the other that pushes us into ethical action is both a linkage to, and a rejection of, her Sartrean existentialist foundations.

In the immediate context of the Algerian war, Beauvoir's very public antiwar stance led to death threats, a partial self-imposed social exile, and the risk of legal repercussions for some of her involvement with the Djamila Boupacha situation. In particular, Beauvoir actually wrote only the introduction of the book *Djamila Boupacha* but signed her name as a co-author with Gisèle Halimi. They did this in order to shield Halimi from the legal risks of revealing material that was crucial to the narrative of torture and legal travesty that the book sought to tell, the publication of which was not legally permitted. Signing as a co-author made Beauvoir equally subject to punishment if the authorities had decided to prosecute.

Even a lifetime of such moments for Beauvoir, and there were many of them, did not lead her to consider herself a woman of action. It seems that Beauvoir saw her own role as working primarily through her writing, which would impel women and men all over the world to think and to act, and to accept responsibility for their actions and inactions. So it is not exactly clear what Beauvoir was trying to say when she denied that she was a woman of action. We might imagine, however, that within Beauvoir's ethical theory, to describe herself in such a way would be to deny the particular content of her undertakings. For Beauvoir, to exist *is* to act. And to be a woman of action is to live one's freedom as a woman. More specifically meaningful to Beauvoir was her vocation as a writer, which led her to seek contact with others who would also take action. This vocation provided a further understanding of the collective responsibility entailed by living an intersubjectively fraught existence.

Postscript re: Djamila Boupacha

As a result of the efforts on her behalf, Djamila Boupacha's case was moved to France. Scrupulous attention was given to fairness in the conduct of Boupacha's case by the judge who heard it in the French city of Caen. The judge repeatedly requested information and pictures of officers from the two prisons for purposes of identification. Military officials repeatedly refused to release such pictures. The persistence of both was taken by Boupacha's advocates as an acknowledgment of the validity of her claims. The judge's requests were consistently denied by the military commanders in France and Algeria on the basis that they might diminish the morale of the soldiers in question and would interfere with their right to confront their accusers (Beauvoir 1962, 171–73). Boupacha was released from prison in May 1962, shortly after the Evian Accords that ended the war were signed. An amnesty law made it impossible to bring her torturers to justice, or to determine their identities (7).

REFERENCES

Arendt, Hannah. [1945] 1994. "Organized Guilt and Universal Responsibility." In *Essays in Understanding: 1930–1954*. New York: Harcourt Brace. 121–32.
———. [1968] 1987. "Collective Responsibility." In *Amor Mundi*. Ed. James W. Bernauer. Boston: Martinus Nijhoff. 43–50.
Beauvoir, Simone de. 1948. *The Ethics of Ambiguity*. Trans. Bernard Frechtman. Secaucus, N.J.: Citadel.
———. 1962. *Djamila Boupacha*. Trans. Peter Green. New York: Macmillan.

————. [1965] 1992. *Hard Times: Force of Circumstance, II.* Trans. Richard Howard. New York: Paragon.

Maran, Rita. 1989. *Torture: The Role of Ideology in the French-Algerian War.* New York: Praeger.

Montreynaud, Florence. 1995. *Le XXe siècle des femmes.* Paris: Editions Nathan.

Ruedy, John. 1992. *Modern Algeria: The Origins and Development of a Nation.* Bloomington: Indiana University Press.

Sorum, Paul Clay. 1977. *Intellectuals and Decolonization in France.* Chapel Hill: University of North Carolina Press.

6   Beauvoir and the Case of Djamila Boupacha

MARY CAPUTI

THE YEARS OF THE ALGERIAN WAR (1954–62) were a troubled period in Simone de Beauvoir's life. The role that France played in its colonial war with Algeria made her painfully aware of those aspects of French culture that she disdained, for it crystallized the middle-class, bourgeois values of a society of which she herself was a product. By now Beauvoir was a renowned philosopher and author in a country whose involvement in the war she openly condemned. Yet she knew her French citizenship constituted a form of tacit complicity in the pathologies of colonial relations. This complicity aggrieved her, and she labeled the war "a personal tragedy" (Murphy 1995, 266).

Beauvoir chose to publicly oppose the Algerian war by involving herself in the legal defense of a twenty-one-year-old Algerian woman named Djamila Boupacha. Boupacha was a member of the Algerian Nationalist Movement, the Front de Libération Nationale (or FLN), and had been charged with seditious activities. Her case, once it came to light, sparked much public outrage. Boupacha had joined the FLN in Algeria after learning that Muslim girls had been debarred from taking their certificates, which would deny them further education and training. To protest this debarring, Boupacha became involved in a number of seditious activities that included stealing medical supplies, collecting intelligence, and hiding a fellow FLN member in her home. By far the most damning offense, however, was the false claim that she had planted a bomb at a university restaurant, which had subsequently been defused before it was to go off. It was this charge that caused Boupacha to be imprisoned and to undergo an horrific ordeal. She was tortured with electrodes and cigarettes, raped with a bottle, gagged, kicked in the ribs, and beaten. She was also hung from a staff over a bathtub "like a shot stag" (Beauvoir and Halimi 1962, 40) and periodically dunked. Under the duress of such treatment, Boupacha confessed to the crime of having planted the bomb. "She was completely cut off from the outside world," wrote Gisèle Halimi, Boupacha's attorney, of her torturous thirty-three-day ordeal in a military prison. "She agreed to sign the whole transcript as it stood" (43). Yet after seeking legal counsel, Boupacha denied any involvement in the bomb-planting affair and insisted that she had confessed only under duress. The eye-witness testimony of two waiters at the university restaurant corroborated her claim of innocence.

Beauvoir was eager to raise public awareness about the mistreatment of a young Algerian woman whose abuse encapsulated so much about the perversions of the colonial relationship. Boupacha's "traumatic defloration" (Beauvoir and Halimi 1962, 12), in other words, served as an allegory for the tragic Algerian experience of French rule. Yet I would argue that Beauvoir's efforts to assist Boupacha also illustrate aspects of her philosophy and her ethics that, as numerous authors note, represent her unique contribution to these fields (Kruks 1995; Vintges 1996; Lundgren-Gothlin 1996; Bergoffen 1997; Tidd 1999; Gothlin 1999; Bauer 2001). Her sensitivity to oppression leads her to insist that we must act on behalf of those struggling against injustice and that we are morally obligated to those less fortunate than we.

Beauvoir and Sartre: "Giving" versus "Freeing"

In *Simone de Beauvoir, Philosophy, and Feminism,* Nancy Bauer argues that even in her earlier texts, Beauvoir was ill at ease with the ethical implications of Sartre's *Being and Nothingness,* which appeared in 1943. Consequently, Bauer maintains, Beauvoir sought to address what she felt were this text's shortcomings. Especially, she felt that in his writings, Sartre could not distinguish between bad faith and genuine oppression, and that he thus failed to appreciate how concrete circumstances can prevent groups of people from demonstrating the freedom, choice, and responsibility that his philosophy so extols. Where Sartre saw the expression of bad faith, she herself saw oppressive relations beyond people's control. Where he saw personal decisions, she saw political circumstances. Increasingly throughout her life, this focus on oppression led her to insist that the philosophy she espoused must bear upon real-life struggles such as that endured by Boupacha. "[H]er motivation stems as much from her dissatisfaction with the ethical implications (and silences) of Sartre's *Being and Nothingness* as it does from her zeal for the book," writes Bauer, who adds that Beauvoir "is trying to express a certain strong disagreement with Sartre's views" (2001, 141), given the latter's confusion of these categories.

In Sartre's case, the problem was grounded in an exaggerated, decontextualized understanding of the human subject and of human agency that discounted the social setting. In *Being and Nothingness,* Sartre's tendency was to privilege the self and its worldview over the social context in which that self is enmeshed, and to speak about such things as freedom, choice, and responsibility as though they were attributes of the subject rather than (at least in part) attributes of an historical, political setting. To be sure, Sartre made much of freedom, choice, and responsibility, but he often failed to appreciate the true constraints that affected how people might exercise these. He overlooked the social context that can weigh heavily on our "free" and "responsible" choices, for how else could he have argued in *Being and Nothingness* that European Jews in the early 1940s could in fact choose to be free, that they were ultimately responsible for their destiny and should take matters into their own hands? (Sartre 1956, 433–556).

By the early 1960s, even Sartre had modified his understanding of how freedom is limited by structures of oppression. Beauvoir, at this time, was taking action on Boupacha's behalf. She agreed to form a team with Halimi, wrote newspaper articles and co-authored a book about the ordeal, and organized and directed the Comité pour Djamila Boupacha. These actions demonstrate her strong conviction that "the concrete possibilities that open up to people are unequal" (Le Doeuff 1995, 62). These differing concrete possibilities mandate that we act on behalf of one another, coming to one another's aid when injustice can be redressed. Thus, Beauvoir did not perceive Boupacha's suffering within the abstract framework that the early Sartre had used when speaking about Jews. Never did she suggest that Boupacha, from her prison cell, could take matters into her own hands. Even in the much earlier *Ethics of Ambiguity,* Beauvoir had written that context has considerable bearing on our situation. "Every man is originally free, in the sense that he spontaneously casts himself into the world. But if we cannot consider this spontaneity in its facticity, it appears to us only as a pure contingency. . . . It is not a matter of retiring into the completely inner and, moreover, abstract movement of a given spontaneity, but of adhering to the concrete and particular movement by which this spontaneity defines itself by thrusting itself toward an end" (Beauvoir 1948b, 25–26).

In order to better appreciate Beauvoir's developing sense of the self's relationship and responsibility to others, I will trace Beauvoir's and Sartre's early disagreements. According to Sonia Kruks, it is the "radical individualism" contained in Sartre's philosophy, but missing from Beauvoir's, that explains why their philosophies comprised differing moral codes (1995, 79–95). This individualism, which for Kruks "amounts to a kind of solipsism" (86), emanates from a fundamentally agonistic relationship between self and other contained in the Sartrean version of Hegel's master and slave dialectic (but missing from Beauvoir's version). Recognizing the radical individualism as presented in *Being and Nothingness* helps us to better understand Sartre's portrayal of the agonistic relationship between self and other. Such an appreciation will allow Beauvoir's far more mutually interdependent relationship between self and other to stand out in relief.

In *Being and Nothingness,* Sartre argues that the free and responsible self, ultimately in control of choosing life's meanings, experiences a relationship with the other marked by struggle and conflict. Sartre relies upon Hegel's conflict between master and slave as he posits the self's task of creating and adhering to those meanings that will allow the immediate world of *en-soi* to assume the transcendent values of one that is *pour-soi*. This will allow the world to be filled with conferred, humanly created meanings for which we are ultimately responsible. For Sartre, this task produces a relationship between self and other that is marked by struggle and conflict, a dynamic reproducing an antagonistic dialectic wherein master and slave battle to the death. Since there is mere "nothingness" between the two, each struggles to reduce the other to a version of oneself, to subsume the other's subjectivity in ways that make it match one's own will and knowledge. Sartre describes the manner in which the interfusion of subject and object is founded on the dynamic of negation, the fact that two coexistent subjectivities are fundamentally at odds. In the following passage there seems little hope of reconciling two agonistic beings into a relationship that is mutually beneficial.

> The Other . . . is presented in a certain sense as the radical negation of my experience, since he is the one for whom I am not subject but object. Therefore as the subject of knowledge I strive to determine as object the subject who denies my character as subject and who himself determines me as object. . . . The Other is the one who is not me and the one who I am not. This not indicates a nothingness as a given element of separation between the Other and myself. Between the Other and myself there is a nothingness of separation. (Sartre 1956, 228–38)

Within the parameters of this universe, two coexistent subjects are by definition in conflict as one contending subjectivity strives to reduce the other to the status of object. Master and slave are locked in a struggle that poses the question of whose subjectivity will prevail, and the interdependence that binds them is seen as a threat to consciousness. At this stage, the relationship between two beings can be marked only by conflict, for the assertion of one consciousness assures the annihilation of the other.

Sartre writes of the other as both a necessary player in the development of self-consciousness and as an impediment to the self's freedom. The other makes possible one's self-definitions by providing the needed recognition—"the Other founds my Being in so far as this being is in the form of the 'there is'" (Sartre 1956, 364)—yet also thwarts the very same. It allows for self-realization even as it countervails against the sovereignty that the self seeks to impose. This polyvalent gesture of affirming through recognition and negating through competition is captured by Sartre when he writes that the other "reveals to me the being which I am" but also forbids me to appropriate that being "or even to conceive it" (363). Thus, while the other retains a hold on the subject's own self-definitions by making recognition possible, it acts as a foil to the desired sovereignty through its own contending subjectivity.

Although essential, the measure of dependency that characterizes our enmeshment with others is viewed by Sartre as a quality that delimits our potential for autonomy and self-direction, a detriment to the manner in which we might exist as sovereign beings. "While I attempt to free myself from the hold of the Other, the Other is trying to free himself from mine," he writes. "While I seek to enslave the Other, the Other seeks to enslave me. . . . Conflict is the original meaning of being-for-others" (1956, 364). Conflict thus keynotes the interconnection between self and other in a dynamic that is both an impediment to the perceiving subject and the *means* necessary to achieve self-realization. What is needed, then, is to make use of the other, to turn the conflict in one's favor.

Hence while the dialectic between self and other is marked by ongoing struggle, it nevertheless provides the necessary venue through which transcendence is reached. For Sartre, the other provides meaning for the subject only when its threat to sovereignty has been overcome; only, in other words, when the subject *appropriates* the other, "absorbing" its subjectivity. The dynamic of negation must proceed as the subject makes use of the other's consciousness, assimilating it for his or her own purposes. "[My freedom] is conceivable only if I assimilate the Other's freedom. Thus my project of recovering myself is fundamentally a project of absorbing the Other" (Sartre 1956, 364). Being freed from the other's grasp through "absorption" contributes vitally to human freedom: I am free once I have annihilated the other's threat to my sovereignty. The other must be overcome, transcended so that the subject may achieve transcendence. A life *pour-soi* assumes the absorption of the other.

Not all scholars agree that the Sartrean reading of Hegel's master-slave, with its emphasis on absorption, amounts to a form of solipsism. Debra B. Bergoffen, for instance, insists that Sartre's dependency on the other disallows a truly solipsistic position, for the experience of transcendence always presupposes a rivaling consciousness, a fellow human being that has been appropriated. For Bergoffen, it is the presence of another consciousness that counts. She writes, "Sartre's analysis of shame, pride, and the caress make it clear that solipsism is untenable, not only because I cannot experience the world as a world without invoking the presence of the other, but also because I cannot fully experience myself outside of the other's presence" (1997, 25). Nevertheless, other scholars argue that, with his emphasis on the absorption of the other, Sartre's philosophy foregrounds *making use* of another for one's own ends, and thus it comes very close to a solipsistic position. Hence, Michele Le Doeuff observes that "[w]hile there is no monadism in Hegel's philosophy when he speaks of consciousness, nor any real risk of solipsism, the French existentialism of the 1940s seems to have taken shape as a subtle play with this risk. . . . When Sartre describes himself as 'a desert island' he reveals a sort of fundamental intuition that is his" (1995, 62).

If we follow Bauer's tracing of solipsism back to Descartes, and if we define this position as one that realizes that my picture of the world "is fundamentally dependent on what goes on in my mind," that sees the need for "taking stock of a certain course of my own thought" (Bauer 2001, 61), then we can agree with Kruks that Sartre's position bears traces of a solipsistic viewpoint. Bauer emphasizes that the Cartesian analysis of solipsism causes us to realize our intellectual solitude, for in taking stock of the course of our own thoughts, we recognize the utter uniqueness of our thought process. We recognize how our thought process affects our intellectual conclusions at which others may never arrive. This intellectual solitude is reflected in Sartre's belief in an essential conflict between self and other, which inspires the statement that he is a "desert island."

Such a statement, of course, exemplifies the radical individualism that Kruks identifies in Sartre's thinking, the individualism that accounts for his philosophy's tendency toward solipsism. According to Kruks, his is an individualism that cannot see beyond itself, and that cannot appreciate how differently others apprehend and experience the world. Thus, Sartre's philosophical need to absorb the other, to assimilate the other's freedom and thereby attain sovereignty, make it difficult for him to understand how the concrete circumstances of another's social reality can impinge on his or her experience of freedom, choice, and responsibility. It is difficult for Sartre to see that not all subjects are in a position to achieve transcendence or to assign meaning to their worlds as he does. Unlike Beauvoir, he was incapable of understanding that not everyone enters into the Hegelian master-slave in the same way and with the same options. For Kruks, this is the problem of *discontinuity* in Sartre's writing, a problem that does not exist in Beauvoir's texts. Kruks writes:

> There is in [Sartre's] work a radical individualism that amounts to a kind of solipsism: each of us construes the meaning of both past and present only from the perspective of our own project. . . . Since situations are each uniquely brought into being by an individual free project, we cannot, for Sartre, conceive of a *general* situation. . . . There is a discontinuity, a hiatus he could not bridge, between . . . the existence of social and historical wholes that appear to have a reality beyond that given to them by each unique individual project. (1995, 86)

It is the way that Sartre conceives his project that obfuscates what Kruks calls "a general situation," a situation created by social and historical forces that surpass and eclipse an individual's perspective. Sartre measures maturity in terms of our absorption of the other, or our ability to assimilate the other's freedom. Yet this presupposes that we are all in a situation to do so: we are free and able to absorb and assimilate in the same way, to achieve sovereignty in the same way. Most important for our purposes, it presupposes that the *conditions* necessary to absorb and assimilate are right for everyone in the same way. The inability to recognize that the other's lived, social conditions may prevent him or her from doing so accounts for the solipsistic discontinuity that caused Sartre to assign bad faith to situations that, for Beauvoir, were in fact, the site of oppression.

Beauvoir's sensitivity to oppression and refusal to see all players as equal in the social arena emanates from her unique reading of Hegel's master and slave dialectic. In this dialectic, she perceived a far less agonistic relationship between two beings whose ethical sense would keep them from engaging in the kind of conflict that he described. The reciprocity that she highlights in her reading of its unfolding proves far more critical of the absorbing and assimilating that Sartre deemed necessary; indeed, these are part and parcel of his mistaken notion of sovereignty that ultimately allow him to be "an island." Despite the common intellectual terrain that the two share, Beauvoir's understanding of the interfusion between subject and object is less characterized by struggle than it is for Sartre.

Beauvoir's reading of the master-slave dialectic permits a far more generous exchange between two beings engaged in struggle. We have seen that Sartre sought to "free" himself from the grasp of the other. Yet for Beauvoir, the interconnection between self and other admits more mutual reciprocity than it does conflict; in *The Ethics of Ambiguity* she insists that the other "gives the world to me" in a gesture that alone allows for our self-definitions. It is "by means of the presence of this world that the Other reveals" that we claim an existence at all (1948b, 55). The giving other whose existence does not thwart my self-understandings is the one whose presence bestows meaning. We therefore need the other and the other's freedom, for it is only this freedom that permits the recognition on which we rely. "One can reveal the world only on a basis revealed by other men," she writes, for "[o]nly the freedom of others keeps each one of us from hardening into the absurdity of facticity" (71). Being freed of the other therefore runs the risk of finding life absurd, of being in a world devoid of meaning, or, as per Sartre, of being in a world comprised of so many "islands."

If the other is a *giving* other, then we wrongly imagine ourselves to be independent, sovereign beings. The quest for sovereignty itself loses meaning once the other's presence takes on generous, life-affirming attributes. We are free only with others who are also free. Unlike Sartre's isolation, Beauvoir's ethics moves into the social arena as it enters a positive relationship with the other who gives. For her, a moral code was something that had meaning only in the social sphere, in relation to others. "The moral code of her ethics reaches into the political arena," writes Karen Vintges, since for Beauvoir "[t]he subject who assumes a moral attitude is socially situated" (1996, 70). The social situation is therefore crucial to Beauvoir's theory in that it alone provides the framework in which such attributes as freedom, choice, and responsibility can be experienced. We recall how, in *The Ethics of Ambiguity*, Beauvoir argued that an attribute of such a freedom, which is spontaneous, is given meaning only in relation to "the concrete and particular movement by which this spontaneity defines itself" (1948b, 26).

Moreover, this emphasis on social context causes Beauvoir's ethics to insist that no subject acts entirely alone. "No project can be defined except by its interference with other projects," she writes. "To make being 'be' is to communicate with others by means of being" (1948b, 71). If the other gives the world to me, there is no need for the act of absorption as described by Sartre, for to "free" oneself from the other is, at bottom, to misconceive one's own freedom. It is to exchange a meaningful life for one that is absurd. Yet even if one did choose absurdity over meaning, Beauvoir fundamentally doubts that one can act in a manner that is absolutely free. Indeed, no one is completely free: "[I]t is true that each is bound to all. . . . Universal, absolute man exists nowhere," she says (112).

This conviction that each is bound to all, together with Beauvoir's insistence that "the concrete possibilities that open up to people are unequal" (Le Doeuff 1995, 62), drives her to insist that, morally, we must act on behalf of one another. This is of course what we witness in the case of Djamila Boupacha, and it represents a difference between her ethical theory and that of Sartre. "In contrast to Sartre, Beauvoir believed that we can and should help others with their lives," writes Vintges. "The aim of her art-of-living ethics is that we have to be a subject who offers others practical assistance in realizing their freedom" (1996, 94). This difference in ethical position became apparent as early as 1940, when Beauvoir argued with Sartre that a woman locked up in a harem is not capable of achieving transcendence.[1] She held, "Basically . . . I was right" (qtd., Kruks 1995, 82). Subsequently, in 1945, she used the following quotation from Dostoevsky's *The Brothers Karamazov* as an epigraph to her second novel, *The Blood of Others:* "Each of us is responsible for everything and every human being" (Beauvoir 1948a).

But how can we respond to *every* human being? And if we do not suffer as they do, what can we authentically know about their suffering? Must we be acquainted with the aggrieved, and know their situation first hand? Let us now turn our attention to complaints registered against privileged persons who act on behalf of the aggrieved, and against Beauvoir in particular as she interceded for Boupacha. Such complaints bring into focus some of the problems that accompany Beauvoir's mandate that we are responsible for helping others, even others with whom we are unacquainted.

Simone de Beauvoir, Entomologist?

On June 2, 1960, *Le Monde* published Beauvoir's article entitled "In Defense of Djamila Boupacha." Its aim was to raise the French public's awareness of Boupacha's ordeal, and to warn the public against becoming acquiescent in the latter's suffering. To become acquiescent in the face of criminal activity,

Beauvoir argued, not only constitutes a scandal but implicates everyone. To remain passive, to get "used to it," is to be complicitous in a crime. She wrote, "The most scandalous aspect of any scandal is that one gets used to it. Yet is seems impossible that public opinion should remain indifferent to the present tragic ordeal of a twenty-one-year-old girl named Djamila Boupacha. ... When the government of a country allows crimes to be committed in its name, every citizen thereby becomes a member of a collectively criminal nation. Can we allow our country to be so described?" (1962, 191–97).

These statements seem consistent with Beauvoir's ethical writings, and they suggest that the Boupacha affair gave Beauvoir the opportunity to act upon her convictions. Nevertheless, at least two people criticized her actions and impugned her motives for becoming involved in the case. They are Frantz Fanon, the Martinican psychoanalyst, and Gisèle Halimi, Boupacha's attorney. Whether directly or by implication, Fanon and Halimi suggested that Beauvoir's actions arose less from a sense of responsibility toward others than from egotistical motives. Here, I would like to pursue these criticisms as a means of highlighting some of the questions that arise when we act on behalf of others. I would especially like to pursue the question of how well we must know the other on whose behalf we intervene. Addressing these questions will give a better sense of what it means to claim, as Beauvoir does, that each of us enjoys a "situated freedom," while simultaneously being "bound to all."

There is first the fact that Fanon fundamentally doubted that "French intellectuals" who took on a colonial cause were truly concerned about the colonized. Julien Murphy (1995) has persuasively argued that Fanon's deep insights into colonial perversions caused him to doubt the sincerity of French public intellectuals acting on behalf of oppressed groups. While it is true that Fanon never attacked Beauvoir personally, he did register criticism against French thinkers who professed concern for those harmed by their nation. Thus, in *Toward the African Revolution,* he wrote: "The gravity of the tortures, the horror of the rape of little Algerian girls, are perceived because their existence threatens a certain idea of French honor. ... Such shutting out of the Algerian ... belongs to that form of egocentric, sociocentric thinking which has become the characteristic of the French" (qtd., Murphy 1995, 282).

Indirectly, then, Fanon suggested that Beauvoir's reasons for being involved in the case were in fact self-serving, protecting the French self-image rather than helping an otherwise unknown, imprisoned Algerian. Fanon's beautiful rendition of colonial dysfunction, delivered also in *Black Skin, White Masks* and *The Wretched of the Earth,* allowed him to read deeply into European "concern" for colonial injustices and to query the nature of hegemonic compassion. In these texts, he discerned the hidden dimensions of seemingly altruistic behaviors and identified a neurotic underpinning to the interactions of those caught in colonial strife. Fanon is well known for his adept appraisal of how those locked into colonial pathologies in fact perpetuate the oppressive dynamic. His texts probe the manner in which colonizer and colonized are entangled in a dysfunctional web that envelops the most sinister dimensions of self-hatred, refuting the claim that either European colonizer or dark-skinned colonized has a clear identity or a resolved mission. Instead, what Fanon perceives is a neurotic entrapment in a mutually destructive *folie à deux.*

In *Black Skin, White Masks,* Fanon expresses serious doubts that colonizing malevolence and colonized suffering are perfect archetypes in binary juxtaposition. Throughout its pages, Fanon doubts that they are monolithic categories of human experience untouched by a more radical confusion. Instead, he sees in the colonial setting a deeply pathological relationship wherein two seemingly antagonistic parties in fact partake of a strange human drama. There is "extreme ambivalence in the colonial situation," he insists (1967, 83), an ambivalence that ensures everyone's enslavement. "The Negro enslaved by his inferiority, the white man enslaved by his superiority alike behave in accordance with a neurotic orientation" (60). This mention of enslavement surely meshes with Fanon's earlier statement regarding egocentric, sociocentric French intellectuals who respond to Algerian oppression only because it hurts *their own* sense of themselves. It describes the tendency to see another's pain in terms only of oneself, to respond to another's suffering out of motives that are ultimately selfish. "And there one lies body to body with one's blackness or one's whiteness," he writes, "in full narcissistic cry, each sealed into his own peculiarity" (45). If we take Fanon's words seriously, then, we might query Beauvoir's intervention on behalf of Boupacha. Who exactly was being helped by her actions? What did she hope to achieve?

To be sure, Fanon's analysis might lead one to see nothing other than an ingrained solipsism contained in Beauvoir's actions. We recall that Kruks defined solipsism as people's inability to perceive "a reality beyond that given to them," such that "each of us construes the meaning of both past and present only from the perspective of our own project" (1995, 86). Fanon's argument against French intellectuals seems to amount to exactly this: they perceive the colonial tragedy only in terms of themselves (they have "a certain idea of French honor") and cannot understand it as someone else's struggle. Fanon's descriptions of the European intellectual's position within this situation might cast doubt on the motivations behind Beauvoir's efforts. Does she, in fact, succeed in devising a theory of oppression that exhorts us to act on each other's behalf? Or might she, instead, by teaming up with Halimi, display a solipsism all her own?

Another question concerning motives is raised by Boupacha's lawyer, Gisèle Halimi. Halimi had taken the initiative in approaching Beauvoir to make the case public, and she commented on how readily Beauvoir accepted. Halimi recalled, "She said 'yes' to my appeal for her help as though it was a matter of course" (Beauvoir and Halimi 1962, 65). Beauvoir subsequently worked hard on Boupacha's behalf. As mentioned, she published essays, organized and directed the Comité pour Djamila Boupacha, and was the co-author, with Halimi, of a book that sought to expose the young woman's torture while condemning the general brutalities of the colonial situation. This book, entitled *Djamila Boupacha: The Story of the Torture of a Young Algerian Girl Which Shocked Liberal France,* contains entries by Beauvoir, Halimi, and various authors who took an interest in the case, including Françoise Sagan. The combined efforts of these women succeeded in slowing the proceedings against Boupacha. The latter's trial finally ended once the Evian agreement was signed between France and Algeria in 1962.

Ultimately, however, Halimi was unhappy about her collaboration with Beauvoir. She was frank in expressing her disappointment in what she saw as Beauvoir's lack of emotional involvement in the case. Although Murphy insists that Beauvoir "risked her reputation on the Boupacha book" (1995, 279), Halimi detected detachment on Beauvoir's part, and a tendency to treat the case in abstract terms. "I expected a sister-in-arms," she wrote, adding that "I discovered more and more an entomologist" (qtd., Murphy 1995, 283). Halimi felt that Beauvoir saw the case as just one among many, an opportunity to oppose the French position in Algeria by making use of Boupacha's ordeal. "For her, Djamila was one victim among thousands, a useful 'case' in the battle against torture and the war" (qtd., ibid.). And, against my claim that Beauvoir's ethical position mandated helping those who suffer oppression, Halimi maintained that Beauvoir took an interest in the case only from a distance: hers was not a hands-on approach that showed deep concern for another's concrete situation, but an abstract appraisal of the situation at large. Halimi asked, "For her, was not understanding the nature of the battle more important than the person at stake?" (ibid.).

Above all, Halimi denounced Beauvoir's unwillingness ever to meet Boupacha, though she had numerous opportunities. Halimi herself was very emotionally involved, meeting with Boupacha often and writing to her when away. Halimi's disappointment with Beauvoir's seeming detachment causes us to wonder what exactly she meant in stating that Beauvoir had readily agreed to assist her. Did Halimi detect a self-serving dimension to Beauvoir's behavior? Might she have accused her of solipsism, when "each of us construes the meaning of both past and present only from the perspective of our own project"? (Kruks 1995, 86). I am insisting that, in her sensitivity to oppression, Beauvoir was incapable of exercising the inveterate self-referencing that contributes to a solipsistic position.

Let me now explain how I would defend Beauvoir against criticisms raised by Fanon and Halimi. I believe that, despite the fact that she never met Djamila Boupacha, Beauvoir's efforts to act on the latter's behalf are consistent with her ethical writings. Her actions demonstrate sensitivity to oppression, as well as her conviction that those in a privileged position must intervene on behalf of those struggling against injustice.

"Acknowledging" and "Recognizing" the Other

The questions raised by Fanon and Halimi imply that, in relation to the Djamila Boupacha affair, Beauvoir's seemingly altruistic actions in fact emanated from selfish motives. Yet in his essay "Knowing and Acknowledging," Stanley Cavell (1976) argues that knowing someone else's pain is different than acting in response to it. The former is a question of knowledge and certainty, while the latter is a choice to respond. When it comes to knowing another's pain, Cavell clearly states that our knowledge will be limited at best. Despite our best efforts, the exact nature of another's suffering will always elude us, for the experience of physical pain has a private dimension that language cannot unveil. Indeed, our inability ever to know fully another's pain represents a philosophical problem, for despite the generalizations we can make about suffering through language, pain is ultimately a private affair. Can we know when and how to intervene against it? "[T]hough it's true that we have compared notes and discovered that we do suffer from the same frightful headache" (Cavell 1976, 244), still one might wonder whether we can be certain that our pain is identical. Cavell remains unconvinced that the nature of suffering translates easily into language: "The answer is, 'Of Course not!'" (ibid.). Thus, we cannot know when action is necessary.

This problem is overcome, however, if we agree to give equal weight to each other's use of language in describing our pain. While the quality of another's suffering may forever elude our grasp, we can understand his or her description of it. Cavell argues that the privacy of pain can be overcome if we grant another's pain based on his or her use of language. "We can disagree in many of our beliefs, but that very disagreement implies that we agree in *the use of words* which express those beliefs" (Cavell 1976, 240, my emphasis). It is important to recognize that understanding what another is saying is not tantamount to providing evidence for it. To understand the reference does not necessitate understanding the content, nor does it require further investigation. If we expect others to allow our statements to stand (at least in ordinary conversation) without painstakingly defining our terms and defending ourselves in every breath, then we must grant as much to others. Cavell writes that "the way you must rely upon yourself as a source of what is said . . . demands that you grant full title to others as sources of that data" (239). In other words, we must allow that another's description of his pain tells the truth about that pain.

According to Cavell, allowing another's use of language to command such authority is what permits us to distinguish *knowing* from *acknowledging*. Our ordinary, everyday exchanges with people demand that we acknowledge what they are saying as true, even without data to confirm things. Everyday speech must proceed on the basis of a trust in words, of a belief that what is being said could be verified were it necessary. More than this, while we often operate in the absence of irrefutable evidence, the fact that we *acknowledge* something in a sense demonstrates that we *do* know it, for to acknowledge it is to behave as though we did. Cavell maintains, "It isn't as if being in a position to acknowledge something is *weaker* than being in a position to know it. On the contrary: from my acknowledging that I am late it follows that I know I'm late (which is what my words say)" (1976, 256–57). Everyday language relies upon our granting authority to things others say in the absence of clear evidence; it relies upon our willingness to acknowledge. Our relations with others depend upon our ability to trust the correspondence between what they mean and what they say.

Cavell is of course aware of the skeptic's claim that words can deceive, that we all know how to dissemble when it suits our needs. And skepticism is an important position to consider. Yet his point is that our ongoing relations must be allowed to bracket skeptical thoughts so that we can acknowledge what others are saying, and thus trust what they say to be true even in the absence of evidence. Where the topic of pain is concerned, what is needed is not more complete knowledge of the other, or more irrefutable evidence about their suffering. Rather, what is needed is the ability to *respond* to the other's statements thanks to our ability to acknowledge the other's claims. As Cavell says, "[W]hen you have twisted or covered your expressions far or long enough, or haven't yet found the words which give the phenomenon expression, I may know better than you how it is with you" (1976, 266). Acknowledging thus allows me to respond to your pain, even if I have never met you.

If we take Cavell's distinction between knowing and acknowledging seriously, then the accusations registered against Beauvoir lose much of their power. The actions that she took on Boupacha's behalf—forming the committee for her, writing newspaper articles, co-authoring the book—need not emanate from complete and detailed knowledge of Boupacha's suffering. Rather, it follows from Cavell's argument that given what the world already knew about Boupacha, what was needed was not more knowledge of her situation but a response to it, not intimate details about her suffering but concrete action to make it stop. Hence, Beauvoir did not need even a superficial acquaintance with Boupacha in order to act on her behalf, for she already held sufficient information about the latter's ordeal to take action.

Patchen Markell agrees with Cavell that aspects of the other's identity, and of the other's suffering, elude us. Yet, in "The Recognition of Politics: A Comment on Emcke and Tully," he approaches this issue from a different angle. Whereas Cavell highlights language's limitations in capturing the private nature of pain, Markell (2000) maintains that, in our efforts to end oppressive relations, language itself may be part of the problem. For Markell, language is not always the ally of progressive politics, for the act of naming oppression and discursively framing the site of pain contains a dangerous underside. He highlights how, in seeking to act politically against oppression, the very terms and expressions we use to define the oppressive situation may actually, ironically, *cause and perpetuate* that same situation. It is not language's limitations that Markell examines, but rather its cunning power to hinder if not foil political progress. In naming and confronting, language can also construct, establish, and solidify what we hope to dismantle. It can further entrench what we seek to root out. "An act of affirmative recognition might also unwittingly strengthen the underlying relations of power and domination that have helped *make* people who they are," he writes, "binding people ever more tightly to the identities that have historically been the instrument of subjection" (498).

Markell thereby insists that the act of recognizing formerly oppressed groups may ironically prolong the oppression that they seek to end; to name is to legitimize, to inscribe within a set of power relations that may in fact be undesirable. Indeed, because language is so fraught with numerous layers of meaning, to inscribe the plight of disadvantaged groups within political

discourse—for instance, to discuss the Algerian sense of inferiority during the war with France—may cause well-meaning actions to backfire as
the search for liberation prolongs oppression. Language can entrench such
groups within a discourse of grievance that does not aid in furthering their
cause but, due to its harmful underside and cunning ability to strengthen existing power relations, proves regressive. Acting on behalf of Boupacha could
thus further inscribe young Algerian women within a panoply of grievances.
It could forever associate them with the many layers of oppression that Boupacha in fact longed to counter. Thus, "if recognition does not simply *know*
its objects but *makes* them" (Markell 2000, 496), were Beauvoir's efforts to
intervene truly altruistic?

Markell never suggests that language's polyvalences need deter political action; he never argues that language's undesired ability to confirm oppressive relations should result in silence or inaction. The great challenge
in agitating on behalf of the oppressed, he admits, is to do so in ways that
necessarily address the social, political, and economic forces that made possible that oppression in the first place—even in light of language's ironies.
Advancing the cause of formerly oppressed groups should in no way play
into the hands of reactionary forces, but, on the contrary, should offer new
ways of framing old problems. Surely this is what Beauvoir was trying to do
for Boupacha as she urged her fellow French citizens not to get "used to" the
latter's suffering, not to acquiesce in a national "scandal." Markell writes:

> Instead of asking only how we can negotiate the dilemmas that the grammar
> of recognition imposes, we should also ask how the grammar of recognition
> itself comes to be imposed as the vocabulary in which redress for injuries
> ... must be pursued. ... [I]f the imperative of pursuing recognition is not
> ontologically necessary but historically and contextually contingent, what
> transformations in the background conditions of contemporary political
> life would make it possible for us to respond *more lucidly than the grammar
> of recognition permits?* (2000, 504)

Like Cavell, Markell thus admits that political action on behalf of the
oppressed proves problematic, for while the existing structures themselves
are part of the problem, it remains difficult to think or act outside of them.
Yet neither he nor Cavell condones subsequent inaction. Whereas Cavell
maintains that limited knowledge of the oppressed other need not make
us passive, Markell similarly insists that our awareness of language's ironies
must never result in political disengagement. "We *cannot but* recognize and

identify ourselves and others," he writes (2000, 504), affirming the need for intervention even when that intervention proves risky. It is only intervention on behalf of the oppressed other that can initiate the process of addressing that very oppression; the "grammar of recognition," as he calls it, can only change as the result of political action.

The arguments of both Cavell and Markell exonerate Beauvoir from the charge of solipsism where the case of Djamila Boupacha is concerned. To use these authors' own terminology, Beauvoir's actions on Boupacha's behalf clearly demonstrate her "acknowledgment" and "recognition" of Boupacha's suffering, and so reveal Beauvoir's desire to come to the latter's aid for her own sake. She may not have known everything there was to about this Algerian woman, and her efforts to raise public awareness about the case may also have brought *her* attention.

Nevertheless, if to acknowledge is to know (as per Cavell), and if we "*cannot but* recognize others" in our efforts to help (as per Markell), then Beauvoir's actions cannot honestly be defined as solipsistic. On the contrary, her actions remain true to her ethical mandate that, because each is bound to all, we must intervene in the fact of political struggle. We are responsible toward those who cannot enjoy the freedom, choice, and responsibility that are open to us, and we must extend the giving gesture toward the other.

NOTES

1. She recalled this later, in *The Prime of Life,* which appeared in 1960 (qtd., Kruks 1995, 82).

REFERENCES

Bauer, Nancy. 2001. *Simone de Beauvoir, Philosophy, and Feminism.* New York: Columbia University Press.

Beauvoir, Simone de. 1948a. *The Blood of Others.* Trans. Y. Moyse and R. Senhouse. New York: Knopf.

————. 1948b. *The Ethics of Ambiguity.* Trans. Bernard Frechtman. New York: Philosophical Library.

Beauvoir, Simone de, and Gisèle Halimi. 1962. *Djamila Boupacha: The Story of the Torture of a Young Algerian Girl Which Shocked Liberal French Opinion.* Trans. Peter Green. New York: Macmillan.

Bergoffen, Debra B. 1997. *The Philosophy of Simone de Beauvoir: Gendered Phenomenologies, Erotic Generosities.* Albany: State University of New York Press.

Cavell, Stanley. 1976. "Knowing and Acknowledging." In *Must We Mean What We Say?* Cambridge: Cambridge University Press. 238–66.

Dostoevsky, Fyodor. 1996. *The Brothers Karamazov.* New York: Random House.

Fanon, Frantz. 1967. *Black Skin, White Masks.* Trans. Charles Lam Markmann. New York: Grove Weidenfeld.

———. 1988. *The Wretched of the Earth.* Trans. Constance Farrington. Berkeley, Calif.: Grove/Atlantic Press.

Gothlin, Eva. 1999. "Simone de Beauvoir's Notions of Appeal, Desire, and Ambiguity and Their Relationship to Jean-Paul Sartre's Notions of Appeal and Desire." In "The Philosophy of Simone de Beauvoir," ed. Margaret A. Simons, special issue, *Hypatia* 14, no. 4 (Fall): 83–95.

Kruks, Sonia. 1995. "Simone de Beauvoir: Teaching Sartre About Freedom." In Simons 1995, 79–95.

Le Doeuff, Michèle. 1995. "Simone de Beauvoir: Falling into (Ambiguous) Line." Trans. Margaret A. Simons. In Simons 1995, 59–65.

Lundgren-Gothlin, Eva. 1996. *Sex and Existence: Simone de Beauvoir and "The Second Sex."* Trans. Linda Schenck. Hanover, N.H.: Wesleyan University Press.

Markell, Patchen. 2000. "The Recognition of Politics: A Comment on Emcke and Tully." *Constellations* 7, no. 4 (December): 496–506.

Murphy, Julien. 1995. "Beauvoir and the Algerian War: Toward A Postcolonial Ethics." In Simons 1995, 263–97.

Sartre, Jean-Paul. 1956. *Being and Nothingness: An Essay on Phenomenological Ontology.* Trans. Hazel E. Barnes. New York: Philosophical Library.

Simons, Margaret A., ed. 1995. *Feminist Interpretations of Simone de Beauvoir.* University Park: Pennsylvania State University Press.

Tidd, Ursula. 1999. "The Self-Other Relation in Beauvoir's Ethics and Autobiography." In "The Philosophy of Simone de Beauvoir," ed. Margaret A. Simons, special issue, *Hypatia* 14, no. 4 (Fall): 163–74.

Vintges, Karen. 1996. *Philosophy as Passion: The Thinking of Simone de Beauvoir.* Trans. Anne Lavelle. Bloomington: Indiana University Press.

CONTRIBUTORS

MARY CAPUTI is professor of political science at California State University, Long Beach, where she teaches political theory. Her research interests are in the areas of feminism, critical theory, psychoanalysis, and postmodernism. She is working on the relationship between gender and Theodor Adorno's negative dialectics. Caputi is the author of *A Kinder, Gentler America: Melancholia and the Mythical 1950s* (2005).

SONIA KRUKS is the Robert S. Danforth Professor of Politics and has served as the director of the women's studies program at Oberlin College. She teaches political philosophy and feminist theory. She is the author of *The Political Philosophy of Merleau-Ponty* (1981), *Situation and Human Existence: Freedom, Subjectivity, and Society* (1990), and *Retrieving Experience: Subjectivity and Recognition in Feminist Politics* (2001).

LORI JO MARSO is associate professor of political science and director of women's and gender studies at Union College. Her book *Feminist Thinkers and the Demands of Femininity* (2006) examines the lives and work of exemplary feminist thinkers (Mary Wollstonecraft, Germaine de Staël, Emma Goldman, and Simone de Beauvoir) to discuss the dilemmas of living and transforming norms of femininity. Marso is also the author of *(Un)Manly Citizens: Jean-Jacques Rousseau's and Germaine de Staël's Subversive Women* (1999) and numerous articles.

PATRICIA MOYNAGH is assistant professor of government and politics at Wagner College, where she teaches political thought and feminist theory. She is completing a book on freedom and the drama of coexistence, a text that also draws on Simone de Beauvoir as a source for thinking through the political dynamics of intimate, societal, and global relations.

KAREN SHELBY is a visiting scholar and lecturer in the Department of Political Science at the University of California, San Diego, where she teaches courses in feminist theory and in gender and public policy. She completed her doctoral studies at Rutgers University in 2004, with a dissertation entitled "Simone de Beauvoir's Theories of Freedom."

EMILY ZAKIN is associate professor of philosophy (and women's studies affiliate) at Miami University. Her primary research interests are in psychoanalysis, Continental philosophy, and political philosophy. She is a co-editor of *Derrida and Feminism: Recasting the Question of Woman* (1997) and is finishing a book manuscript entitled "Tragic Fantasies: The Birth of Polis and the Limits of Democracy."

INDEX

abortion, Beauvoir on illegality of, 45

abstract good, agenda of, 42

abstract universal: failure of, 43; Irigaray and Kristeva as suspicious of, 31

action, 87; Beauvoir and Arendt compared regarding, 7; Beauvoir on call to political and ethical, 106; Beauvoir on dependency of upon situation and politics, 104; decisions about, 98; disclosure of meanings revealed in each person's, 94; as ethical, 7; ethical meanings of in political contexts, 93; as failure to act, 94–95; and freedom, 7; as inaction, 99; as linked to collective responsibility, 93; on other's behalf, 8; risks of, as constitutive of Beauvoir's politics, 4

adventurer, the, described by Beauvoir, 97

agency, 5, 66–67; Foucault's denial and presuppositions of, 56

Algeria: Beauvoir's opposition to France's colonial retention of, 93; France's collective responsibility for, 101; France's colonial intervention of as conditioning situation, 3; mid-twentieth-century colonial rule over, 6

Algerian nationals, 6

Algerian War for Independence (1954–62), 6, 103; Beauvoir's eliciting French support for, 6; Beauvoir's feelings about, 93;

French responsibility for, 106; response to, by Beauvoir and fellow citizens, 94

Algérie française, Beauvoir's opposition to, 101

Algren, Nelson, 77–78; Beauvoir's passionate love with, 77; feminists' reactions to Beauvoir's letters to, 77

ambiguity, 38; Beauvoir on recognition of condition of, 96; Beauvoir's thesis about subjectivity as nonidentity and, 5; clarity of woman's embodiment of, 78; as fundamental to ethics, 43; as giving rise to freedom, 43; human condition and, 13, 94; at political level, 43

anti-colonial French intellectuals, Fanon's doubts about sincerity of, 118–19

anti-essentialist position, Beauvoir's identification with, 11

antiwar agenda, Beauvoir's support of, 104

apathy, during Algerian War, 103–4

Arendt, Hannah, 7, 19–20, 22, 100, 103; on bourgeois understanding of world, 106; on failure of engagement in public realm and modernity, 101; on Holocaust and judgment, 104; on political import of guilt and responsibility, 100; on popularizing Kant's theory of judging, 12; on responsibility for atrocities, 106

artist and writer, the: Beauvoir on role of,

The University of Illinois Press
is a founding member of the
Association of American University Presses.

———————————————————————

Composed in 10.5/13 Adobe Minion
by Jim Proefrock
at the University of Illinois Press
Manufactured by Thomson-Shore, Inc.

University of Illinois Press
1325 South Oak Street
Champaign, IL 61820-6903
www.press.uillinois.edu